the charity of British rugby

WOODEN SPOON SOCIETY

# RUGBYWORLD'03

## Editor
## Ian Robertson

## Photographs
## Colorsport

# Queen Anne Press

A QUEEN ANNE PRESS BOOK

© Lennard Associates Limited 2002

First published in 2002 by
Queen Anne Press, a division of
Lennard Associates Limited
Mackerye End
Harpenden, Herts AL5 5DR

A catalogue entry is available from the British Library

ISBN 1 85291 646 X (hardback)
ISBN 1 85291 647 8 (paperback)

Production Editor: Chris Marshall
Cover Design/Design Consultant: Paul Cooper
Reproduction: Alan Clark at Prism Digital
Printed and bound in Slovenia

The publishers would like to thank Colorsport for providing most of the photographs for this book.

The publishers would also like to thank AllsportUK, David Gibson (Fotosport), Inphopics, and Chris Thau for additional material.

# With over 100,000 product lines there's only one merchant who can satisfy all your building requirements.

**Travis Perkins is pleased to support
The Wooden Spoon Society Rugby World 2003**

- Over 570 branches nationwide
- 100,000 product lines
- Tool Hire available at selected branches

**www.travisperkins.co.uk**

For information on our network of branches nationwide call
our Customer Careline on **0800 389 6611.**

**Travis Perkins**

# Contents

# FOREWORD

## by HRH THE PRINCESS ROYAL

HRH The Princess Royal
Royal Patron

**Wooden Spoon Society**

BUCKINGHAM PALACE

I am pleased to tell you that Wooden Spoon's beneficial influence on disadvantaged children continues to grow. In a 24 hour period, during February 2002, the charity distributed £563,000 to five projects throughout the UK ranging from a Centre for Autism in Scotland, to a Cystic Fibrosis Unit in Liverpool, to a Wooden Spoon Society Special Purpose Boat presented to the West of England School for Children with Little or No Sight, which is based in Exeter.

The charity celebrates twenty years of supporting disadvantaged children on 19th March 2003. From serendipitous beginnings, in 1983, when five rugby fans travelled to Dublin and came away with a wooden spoon to mark the defeat of the English, the organisation has grown to become a charity working in 29 regions throughout the UK. "Winning" the wooden spoon has never before had such a positive impact on the lives of disadvantaged children.

I'd like to take this opportunity to congratulate the staff, volunteers, Trustees and the thousands of supporters of the charity in reaching this landmark anniversary. I look forward to seeing the charity continue to thrive in the next twenty years.

Anne

# Wooden Spoon Society
### the charity of British rugby
# – 20 Years Young!

Royal Patron:       HRH The Princess Royal
Patrons:            Rugby Football Union • Scottish Rugby Union
Welsh Rugby Union • Irish Rugby Football Union

'It's not what we do … it's what we do with the money!'

Who would have thought that we would have hit a 20th birthday? On 19 March and 16 September 1983 two events took place that would shape a new organisation which would go on to have a positive impact on the lives of disadvantaged children and young people for the next 20 years. No, it wasn't a large company declaring that end-of-year profits or mid-term bonuses would be donated to children (that comes later!). It was a weekend away to watch rugby, followed in September by a golf day and a rugby dinner.

When England lost to Ireland in March 1983 in Dublin, a group of English lads accepted with grace, on behalf of their compatriots, the Wooden Spoon given by their Irish friends and acquaintances in Ballsbridge. If it wasn't for the English team's poor performance the charity may never have started! The defeat to Ireland completed a torrid season for England, who recorded losses against all their Five Nations opponents.

On the journey back to 'the far side' the proposal to play golf for the 'Spoon' attracted the support of fellow English supporters together with the pilot and crew of the British Airways flight. When

LEFT The original Spoon Council and partners at the opening of the Solihull Project in 1992, our first project to cross the £500,000 spend barrier.

RIGHT Starmers stirring again!

BELOW RIGHT Fred Hucker, Vic Durling, Alan Minter and Peter Scott present the fruits of our first project to the headmistress of Park School, Aylesbury.

those 127 like-minded individuals attended that first golf day at Farnham Golf Club in September 1983, little did they know what they were starting. A day's golf, all well and good; an evening's entertainment, even better; a rugby influence, terrific! But what caused that evening to take off?

It was for this golf day that the now immediately recognisable Wooden Spoon tie was first designed. Some 50 ties were made up incorporating the colours of the Four Home Nations, and these would be sold to help to pay the green fees. The ties were quickly purchased, but not all were necessarily worn! One participant was heard to say that he would certainly not be able to wear such a horrendous tie (repeated later on national TV by Nigel Starmer-Smith himself. For shame!) and thus auctioning it off for a charitable cause seemed a reasonable course of action. From such humble beginnings ...!

Little was it anticipated that at the end of a fantastic and somewhat different golf day a sum of £8450 would be raised, enabling the embryonic Spoon to purchase a minibus for the Park Special Needs School in Aylesbury. Our first project, and completed on Day One! Reflecting on such a wealth of goodwill, the organising committee thought that it would be well worth doing it all over again the following year, and this is precisely what happened.

In those first few months certain parameters were laid down. There was agreement to form a charity, naturally it would be called the Wooden Spoon Society. The charity would be run in a professional manner with profits donated to disadvantaged children and young people. It was also agreed that the charity would adhere to the original ethos of having fun at the same time as raising money.

As well as repeating the golf day, we would organise a ball that would have the advantage of involving wives and girlfriends in our newly formed endeavour (hence the Annual Ball), and to embrace our rugby beginnings we would celebrate St George's Day at the Rose Room, Twickenham.

In addition to all this, there were certain Welshmen at Farnham that first year who felt that celebrating an English defeat was no bad thing! A Welsh National Committee of Spoon was formulated, as indeed were the quite extraordinary Radyr Golf Days followed by first-class Welsh Pre-Match Luncheons. Suffice it to say that for the latter the invitations to attend informed the ungodly that the reception for the luncheon (*sic*) was at 12.30 for 6.00 p.m!

In April 1984 the first of the legendary St George's Nights at the Rose Room was held, and these became tremendous fun and fund-raising evenings. That November, at the Regent Crest Hotel, the first Spoon Ball was held. The Spoon Ball is now, we are proud to say, the biggest event that the

DINNER DANCE

SOUVENIR BROCHURE

LONDON HILTON on PARK LANE

Friday 22nd November 1985

London Hilton on Park Lane has held, or holds, in any year.

Such were the early days of the Wooden Spoon Society and such they remained for the remainder of the 1980s. By 1990 we were holding five to six events a year, spread across Cardiff, Birmingham, Twickenham, Farnham and London. Great fun, of great benefit, but still of moderate aspirations compared with today's national charity. In 1990 it was decided to appoint a part-time administrator to regularise the voluntary activities of the founder members, and Jill and David Roberts undertook the task on the very much part-time basis of one day a month.

It was around the same time that Peter Brommage, the sadly missed treasurer of the Rugby Football Union, suggested that the Wooden Spoon Society might wish to come under the umbrella of the RFU as an affiliated and recognised charity. However, the Trustees felt that this would disenfranchise the Celtic fringe, of which the Welsh Wooden Spoon and our sister society in Ireland, the Irish Wooden Spoon Society, had been a massive part (Scottish Spoon came later to the party), and thought that it would perhaps be better if we could seek RFU patronage rather than recognition. Within a year we had the Four Home Unions as our Patrons and were especially proud some four years later when Her Royal Highness the Princess Royal agreed to become our Royal Patron.

Growth thereafter took place very quickly in terms of activities across the UK, and the strong press of opinion felt that a regional development programme was very much required by the ever-increasing membership. In 1993 we celebrated our tenth birthday in style, and now we have, in what seems a remarkably quick time, reached another milestone, our 20th birthday.

Over the intervening years, region upon region joined Family of Spoon, and our activities and growth maintained a steady upward curve. The regional growth, however, did

not simply happen but was the result of a perceived and dedicated plan.

It was realised early in the development of the regional structure of Wooden Spoon that it was difficult fund-raising on a national basis when regional preferences are so strongly promoted. It was hard to encourage people in Liverpool to raise funds for Cardiff, or for Spoon in Edinburgh to seek to support a project in Birmingham. London, of course, faced even greater deprivation than the provincial fringe – nobody, but nobody, wanted to support London!

Therefore a policy was put in place for Local Funds for Local Projects. Furthermore the Trustees (by now known as the Council – there's posh!) decreed that not only should every penny raised locally be spent locally, but that the national fund-raising by the core staff team would be used to double these locally raised funds on a pound for pound basis. Have fun and at the same time Double Your Money! What a recipe for success!

*Quelle différence*! What great motivation for a local committee and what a great incentive to make a real difference in the community. Spoon blossomed and exploded from there, culminating in today's 30 Regional Committees and three National Committees of Scotland, Wales and Ireland and more than 7000 subscribing members. It has become a national charity – but one working very much at a local level.

However, during all this growth and transition we have never forgotten our roots, firmly placed between the gaps in the duckboards around the rugby pitches of the Four Home Unions. We have also left our mark on the game. The wheelchair enclosures at Twickenham were quickly followed by those at Murrayfield and later on at the Millennium Stadium in Cardiff. We

---

*ABOVE LEFT* One of the four Spoon Bars at Twickenham.

*LEFT* The Spoon Wheelchair Bar at Twickenham.

*ABOVE RIGHT* The Wooden Spoon Bar at the Millennium Stadium, Cardiff.

*RIGHT* Our Royal Patron opens the Wooden Spoon Wheelchair Terrace at Murrayfield.

have developed a rugby training programme for those less advantaged (New Image Rugby); provided rugby opportunities for the Inner Cities (under the RFU Social Inclusion Programme); and provided many other inspired rugby initiatives, not least of which is the book that you are now reading – *Wooden Spoon Society Rugby World*, now in its seventh year of publication.

Our strength and purpose, however, have been to convert the funds derived from our rugby and other activities to benefit children and young people disadvantaged in life. We have supported work that takes on cancer, cystic fibrosis and autism. We have tried to have a positive impact on disability in all its forms and comforted the sick and needy whenever we have been able to do so. We have assisted children and young people who are disadvantaged socially, physically or mentally.

We have met all these foes with good humour and much enjoyment. We have created events and activities that have challenged our physical frailties and made great demands on our sporting and social prowess.

We are driven by a collective ambition to see Wooden Spoon Society continue to grow in stature and thereby continue to have a positive impact on disadvantaged children and young people throughout the United Kingdom. If you have enjoyed reading about our history and it strikes a chord with you, then why not be a part of our future?

Full details and membership information can be obtained on our website (www.woodenspoonsoc.org.uk) or please contact:

The Spoon Office
0870 870 0510 (tel); 0870 870 0511 (fax)
charity@woodenspoonsoc.org.uk (e-mail)

**ABOVE** The Spoon Cystic Fibrosis Unit in Broad Green, Liverpool.

**BELOW** The Wooden Spoon Family Cancer Care Unit at Stoke Mandeville.

**BELOW LEFT** The Spoon Child Development Centre at Lambeth, South London, our £3.1 million Millennium Project.

# COMMENT
# & FEATURES

# Jason Robinson
# the Best is Yet to Come

### by PAUL ACKFORD

'It's knowledge that I need, but that only comes with time and matches. I'm happy where I am but not content that I can sit back. I know I need to improve.'

The most frightening thing about Jason Robinson is that he is going to get better. England's most dazzling recruit from rugby league, the original twinkletoes, is a self-confessed ignoramus when it comes to rugby union.

It's not false modesty. The bloke hasn't got the faintest idea. Where to stand? What to do? It's a mystery to him. 'I didn't know why decisions were given or what penalties were for when I first played,' Robinson confessed. 'I didn't have a clue. Sometimes I wasn't able to react as quickly as I would have liked because I couldn't anticipate the consequence of a decision. Thankfully, there were other people in the team who knew what was going on, so I just followed them.'

So much for the theory that playing for your country is hard won, that it requires a lengthy apprenticeship in clubland and 20-plus Tests to settle in before familiarity brings understanding which leads to dominance. Robinson, with only a paltry 11 England appearances to his name, has debunked that myth good and proper.

His lack of knowledge is hardly surprising when one compares his 18-month union apprenticeship with the 16 years and 302 games, including 12 Great Britain caps, he managed in league. No wonder he confesses to being a touch out of his depth in his new environment, even allowing for the closeness of the two codes.

Yet, if the first response to Robinson is amazement that he can be so staggeringly effective in what are still alien surroundings, then the second is an absolute conviction that he will improve. Everyone who has met or worked with him speaks of his God-given talent and his professional attitude.

*RIGHT* Jason Robinson, playing at full back, pulls away from Wallaby lock Justin Harrison during England's 21-15 victory over world champions Australia at Twickenham in November 2001. Robinson continued at full back for England during the 2002 Six Nations Championship.

Adrian Hadley, Robinson's erstwhile director of rugby at Sale, is still gobsmacked at his visits to the club when he was on Wigan's books. 'Before Jason had signed a contract he would come to Sale and watch videos of games with me. He was full of questions. Why are they doing that? Why is he standing there? He also made sure that he had the pen pictures of all the playing and coaching staff so that when he came to his first training session he could call everyone by their first names. On his first away trip he was up the front of the bus doing the DJ bit, playing some of his soul tunes. He made a good impression.'

Brian Ashton, England's attack coach last season, remembers Robinson from their four months together at Bath in 1996. 'His ability to change from a lateral direction to a forward one is quite remarkable. It's the combination of agility and supreme strength that makes him so elusive. Doing plyometrics, jumping off a box straight-legged up into the air again, he was way, way above the Bath players. They were staggered. He was a quiet sort, an incredibly private man, but a fantastic professional. He used to ring me on a Sunday after a game wanting to know about his performance from a tactical and technical point of view. He had thought about the game, made notes and then

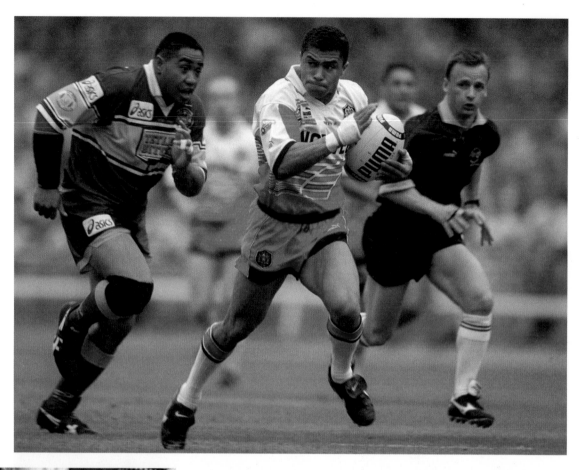

sought an opinion. It made me work twice as hard as a coach because I had to study the tape from his point of view, not just the team's, but it was worth it.'

Robinson wasn't always so diligent. A born-again Christian, his relationship with rugby has altered dramatically. 'I changed about five years ago. Before, I was naive, immature, sucked into all that surrounds the game, the drinking and clubbing, the nice cars. I was brought up to think that if you have money you won't have problems, but I found that the more I got, the more problems I got, and it reached a stage where I didn't want to live that life any more.

*ABOVE* On his way to the man of the match award as Wigan beat Leeds 30-10 in the 1995 Rugby League Challenge Cup final.

*LEFT* Robinson runs out for his Lions Test debut v Australia at the Gabba, Brisbane, in 2001. Within moments of the start, he had scored the Lions' first try, scorching past Chris Latham down the left wing.

*RIGHT* Jason Robinson, Zurich Player of the Year 2001-02, as seen by John Ireland

*FOLLOWING PAGE* Stepping inside Pontypridd's Gareth Wyatt during the Sale Sharks' Parker Pen Shield final triumph at the Kassam Stadium in 2002.

'I discovered that it didn't matter what car I had because I was always chasing another, or what relationship I was in because I always wanted something else. I realised that was shallow and that there was no fulfilment in that way of life. I've found peace and fulfilment in my faith. I don't have to chase those things any more.'

Maybe it is this new outlook which has enabled him to cope with the fresh challenge. 'The game doesn't get the better of me any longer. In the old days I had an extremely short fuse and if a fight flared up on the pitch I would be in there. I let things get to me. The game doesn't get to me any more. I suppose those closest to you can aggravate you more than anything else. Sometimes my wife will get the backlash of me being away from home for a while or being tired from training, but it's rare I get mad or lose my cool.'

When Robinson first burst on to the scene there were rumours that some of the current stars resented his indecently hasty promotion – upstart league convert muscling into new and valuable territory. That was the theme; not that it bothers the great man.

'There shouldn't be any bitterness because I've come from rugby league. It might have been different if I had gone in with the wrong attitude, but I'm aware I've got a lot to learn. I've brought a dose of healthy competition into the squad.'

So what now for the 27-year-old? 'It's knowledge that I need, but that only comes with time and matches. I'm happy where I am but not content that I can sit back. I know I need to improve. I will do it step by step, and if it means making mistakes then sometimes that's the best way to learn. If I knew all the rules it would help. I suppose I'm around 75 per cent of where I want to be.'

And that from Zurich's player of the season and a British Lion to boot. Frightening.

# Rugby and Technology
## Keeping Ahead of the Pack
### by ALASTAIR HIGNELL

On the field of play, rugby remains a contest of skill, strength and speed, yet off the field, technology has been embraced. These three articles explore its impact, both in enhancing game analysis and in providing resources via the Internet.

'I can tell you, but then I'd have to kill you.' When Kyran Bracken, then of Bristol, wound up a television interview with that explanation of how the Memorial Ground outfit would secure a first ever Premiership win over Bath, he was just being mischievous. When the RFU refuse to co-operate on a feature about the new game analysis technology they are developing, you have to hope they are guided by the same motivation.

Whether, after announcing the existence of a system, developed with the aid of those entrusted with the security of the realm, they are now being properly protective or pathetically paranoid, or something in between, is open to question. In rugby, however, the fear of espionage is ever-growing – there are some, for instance, who believe that the Lions lost last summer's series in Australia only because the Wallabies had 'cracked' the tourists' line-out code. Training sessions, which had once attracted thousands of awestruck schoolchildren eager to see their heroes in the flesh, are now closed. In what was once described as the great global freemasonry of rugby, secrets are jealously guarded. Disinformation is as important as information. However, at great risk to my own personal safety, I can reveal what was in the public domain about Pro-zone, the aforementioned high-tech system, before the messengers were gagged.

'If an England player so much as picks his nose at Twickenham, we'll know about it.' That's the promise of Tony Biscombe, match analyst at the RFU. Biscombe and his men no longer have to worry about what the television screens are showing. They have a bank of their own cameras as well as a set of highly sophisticated computers to track every England player for every second of the 80-plus minutes they spend on the pitch at Twickenham.

At the end of the match, Tony's back-room boys reckon they'll be able to tell how far each player has run, and at what speed. They reckon to be able to count the number of rucks he has entered, as well as the number of tackles

he has made. At the flick of a switch, they can show him the lines he has run and the angles he has taken. And, of course, they can highlight how many times he's stopped to attend to his nostrils ...

Why only a handful of cameras, when there are, or should be, 15 England players on the pitch at any one time? The answer is that instead of allocating one camera to one player Biscombe's technology provides a computerised bird's-eye view of the whole pitch, with all the players on screen all the time, while simultaneously offering up four different side-on views. A player is first of all 'tagged' for the benefit of the bird's-eye view camera by a human 'intervention' expert. Each dot on the pitch therefore has a symbol and an identity, which it retains (with the intervention expert checking from time to time that the computer has got it right) even when 16 players go down in a set scrum or an unspecified number enter a maul and all the top-shot camera can see is a mass of shapes. As a result, Biscombe and his boffins can provide a series of graphics for each player, showing each and every movement he makes, the speed at which he makes it and the distance he has travelled. They can tell how much of a game the player spends at top speed and how long he has to recover between bursts of extreme effort – all valuable information for the fitness and conditioning experts.

The coaches benefit from actual pictures, provided not just by the broadcasters but by a series of specially positioned Pro-zone cameras. When a player moves from one section of the pitch to another, he is

*ABOVE* The RFU cameraman has specific instructions at set pieces. At the scrum, the requirement is to show how all 16 forwards engage.

*RIGHT* Robbie Morris had benefited from studies of Puma scrummaging techniques when he faced Argentina on the 2002 tour.

*PREVIOUS PAGE* Could the Lions have been compromised by Wallaby line-out code breakers, as some have claimed?

'passed' from one camera/computer to another. 'Events' in which he is involved are logged by both the intervention expert and the top-shot computer, which is so sophisticated that it needs only a little help to distinguish between a ruck/maul and a scrum, a knock-on and a forward pass. Synchronised time codes enable these events to be recognised as a slice of televised action and as a graphic.

By the end of the match each such event has been identified and labelled. All events of one type (scrums, line outs, goal-kicks, etc) can then be grouped together on the computer and edited into a package for near immediate consumption by coaches or players. In fact, Biscombe aims to have a CD in the hands of each of England's specialist coaches by the time they report for work on a Monday morning.

Besides the pictures provided by the broadcasters and his own tracker cameras, Biscombe can also call on the services of his own special cameraman, whose job is to film from certain specified angles at every set piece. At the line, for instance, Biscombe wants to see both thrower and jumper in the same shot. At the set scrum, the brief is to show how all eight forwards of each side engage and shove.

The evidence he produces is invaluable for the specialist coaches like scrummage expert Phil Keith-Roach. On the recent tour of Argentina he was able to spend quality time with the likes of highly promising but still inexperienced prop Robbie Morris, poring over a specially compiled CD-ROM of 'The Pumas' Greatest Scrummaging Hits'. Biscombe's cameraman was also able to show England's line-out jumpers how Argentina's two hookers, Fred Mendez and Mario Ledesma, 'gave away' when and where they were about to throw the ball.

By the same token, Biscombe's work can be overtly motivational. Each player can be given a CD-ROM of his greatest moments – as well as his worst ones – set to his favourite music. Jonny Wilkinson by all accounts reckons that studying himself making a succession of successful kicks at goal is a vital part of his mental rehearsal for each match.

Laptop computers, and the ability to use them, are as vital to today's England player as a good pair of boots, but, thank the Lord, only the latter is much use once the white line that borders the pitch has been crossed. Having the best plan is not necessarily enough – Bristol never beat Bath when Kyran Bracken was around. Having the best technology is equally only part of the story. However, should England win the World Cup next autumn, we'll all be ready to hail the secret weapon that gave them the edge.

**NEXT**

# Rugby Websites North of the Equator

## by ALASTAIR HIGNELL

In the paperless world of the Internet, it's still difficult to see the rugby wood for the trees. There are so many sites out there, that it would be impossible to review them all. Some have the bells and whistles of video clips and audio interviews, while others are pretty basic. Some try to be all things to all men and women; others are aimed at a very narrow clientele. All, however, stand or fall by the efficiency of those responsible for feeding in the information, and the regularity with which they do so. All sites need to be updated regularly. Not all of them are. The best sites are very, very good, providing reliable, up-to-the-minute information and any number of cross references. Nevertheless there are still a significant number who need to try harder.

## 1. International sites

Each of the Six Nations has a sophisticated, well-thought-out site, with a front page packed with eye-catching offers, information and headlines. At first glance alone, the Ireland, Wales and Italy sites seem more worthy, less attractive, while the RFU site, with its moving banners and flashing list of contents, just edges out the offerings from Scotland and Wales. Alone of all these sites, rfu.com offers interactive video highlights on the front page, with a mouth-watering selection of clips from recent matches on the menu – for a fee.

The International Rugby Board has its own site as well, which should in theory provide the most authoritative picture of results and fixtures around the world, as well as an indication of how and what the powers that be are thinking. In practice, though, it struggles to keep abreast of everything that is happening, and when. If you had consulted the IRB's fixtures as late as the beginning of June, for instance, you would have been under the impression that England were playing Argentina on the 29th. The match was actually scheduled, and played, a week earlier. Errors like that undermine the credibility of a site. The game's governing body needs to get it right.

*A section of the Planet Rugby home page, showing various news sections including Planet Rugby, Zurich World Rankings, top stories about "No Jonah, but Umaga will start", "Bath pull plug on Connors", "Waratahs win the Tuqiri race", and "Asselin is Sevens withdrawal". Navigation menu includes Return to Home, Latest News, News Search, By Country, Free Email News, Columnists, Your Say, Fixtures, Results, Tournaments, Laws & Refs, Coaching, Rugby on TV, Archive / Players, Photo Galleries, Rugby Lookalikes, Fun & Downloads, Rugby Shop, Betting on Rugby, Message Board, Advertise with us, Contact Us, Rugby Quiz, Rugby Audio.*

**ABOVE** A section of the Planet Rugby home page, available at www.planet-rugby.com.

## 2. Clubs

Every self-respecting club in the land has its own website, and in general the Premiership clubs offer a slick, easy-to-use service for their fans. But first impressions count and while Wasps provided the most arresting opening image – a scary-looking insect seemingly breaking out of the screen – Northampton's title page was dull and Leicester's, in mid-July, was still advising members how to pick up tickets for the Heineken Cup final that had taken place two months previously. While few clubs missed a trick in terms of trying to plug their own merchandise, only a couple could offer the opportunity to purchase season tickets online. Without exception, these sites provide a wealth of statistical information – more than enough to settle the most abstruse argument between anoraks.

## 3. Newspapers

And, thanks to the Internet, those worthy gentlemen can compare and contrast the coverage provided by the national newspapers. The *Telegraph*, *Guardian*, *Times*, *Independent* and *Daily Mail* all 'publish' on the net. Whereas a rugby fan once would have had to wade through acres of newsprint, he or she now has only to toggle a switch to have all the rugby pages on screen. If a fan's French is good enough he or she can also add *L'Equipe* to the bookmark list. The French sports paper is simply the best there is, both for coverage and for ease of research.

## 4. General

Sometimes, though, it is preferable to visit sites specifically designed for the Internet. These are more often genuinely interactive, offering the chance not only to see video clips and hear audio files but also to participate in chats with players, coaches and other fans. The Sky site even features their Stuart Barnes as a kind of agony aunt – publishing extracts from their viewers' letters and their pundit's replies. Both Sky's site and the award-winning BBC Online are outstanding, while the Zurich Premiership site and scrum.com deserve honourable mentions. However, the most comprehensive of them all is Planet Rugby, a one-stop rugby shop which not only breaks stories from across the globe but also supplies a full and wholly reliable statistical service.

Those are just the sites that I have bookmarked. It is by no means a full list, more a snapshot of what is out there. New sites are springing up all the time, with ever more intriguing sections. Researching this article, I came across a hitherto unknown address, Web Rugby.com. The title page suggests that it aims to be a sort of gateway to other sites, providing links, for instance, to sites in all the known rugby-playing countries. There are sections on coaching and refereeing, as you'd expect, but most intriguing of all is a section on leisure, promising information on betting, board games and rugby songs. The Internet truly has something for everyone!

---

### BOOKMARKS

**International**
IRB: www.irfb.com
England: www.rfu.com
Scotland: www.sru.org.uk
Wales: www.wru.co.uk
Ireland: www.irishrugby.ie
France: www.ffr.fr
Italy: www.federugby.it

**Zurich Premiership**
Bath: www.bathrugby.com
Bristol Shoguns: www.bristolshoguns.co.uk
Gloucester: www.gloucesterrugbyclub.com
NEC Harlequins: www.quins.co.uk
Leeds Tykes: www.leedsrugby.com
Leicester Tigers: www.tigers.co.uk
London Irish: www.london-irish.com
London Wasps: www.wasps.co.uk
Newcastle Falcons: www.newcastle-falcons.co.uk
Northampton Saints: www.northamptonsaints.co.uk
Sale Sharks: www.salesharks.com
Saracens: www.saracens.com

**Selected media**
Planet Rugby: www.planet-rugby.com
Scrum.com: www.scrum.com
Web Rugby.com: www.webrugby.com
Zurich Premiership: www.zurichrugby.co.uk
Sky: http://msn.skysports.com/skysports/home
BBC Online: http://news.bbc.co.uk
*Telegraph*: www.telegraph.co.uk
*The Guardian*: www.guardian.co.uk
*The Times*: www.timesonline.co.uk
*Independent*: www.independent.co.uk
*Daily Mail*: www.dailymail.co.uk
*L'Equipe*: www.lequipe.fr

# Rugby Websites Down Under

## by RAECHELLE EDWARDS

The emergence of the Internet and its increasing sophistication has been a revelation for sports fans around the world. No longer do we struggle to find out scores from matches we've missed or have a longing for information from other cities and other countries. The click of a mouse and the tap of a keyboard and *voilà*, a plethora of rugby is at our fingertips.

When it comes to rugby, the best assets of the Internet include enabling a user to access live scores in an era when many matches are confined to a pay television, cable audience. The emergence of on-demand video means that we can play back our favourite tries and interviews with players online. The Internet is a great way to chat with the international rugby community and trade views in forums and debates. It also provides the opportunity to get closer to the players by sending them personalised e-mails and asking questions of the stars in celebrity chat rooms. And who can resist the opportunity to procrastinate at the office to check out breaking rugby news – from who is playing on the weekend, to the latest injuries, to which players have signed with new clubs, to the betting odds?

In the southern hemisphere, coverage of rugby on the Internet includes the official websites of the Australian, New Zealand and South African Rugby Unions as well as Rugby Heaven and Eero Tarik. Find out how they rate:

**1. Australian Rugby Union official site**  *Web address*: www.rugby.com.au

*Content*: The major sections of this site include Wallabies, Waratahs, Reds, Brumbies, Super 12, Club Rugby, Tri-Nations, Bledisloe Cup, Sevens, Under 21s, Under 19s, Youth Rugby and Women's Rugby.

The site has areas such as player profiles, a calendar of events and ticketing information as well as competitions, screensavers and an online shop from which users can purchase official merchandise. There are also links to relevant sites such as corporate hospitality and official travel agents. This site is a mouthpiece for the Australian Rugby Union with relevant information but no real excitement – it serves its purpose. *Rating*: 6/10

*Dynamic content*: Real-time score updates during Wallabies Tests with a running text commentary, and breaking news generated by the Australian Rugby Union (press releases) and Australian Associated Press (wire service). *Rating*: 8/10

*Multimedia*: Limited audio and video content. *Rating*: 1/10

*Final comment*: There is a lot of content on this site. It covers a broad range of rugby in Australia and incorporates most material a user would expect from the official Australian Rugby Union site but could be improved by interactive elements such as chat, games and video. The Australian Rugby Union would also benefit from getting the players more involved in the site as a method of communication with their fans.

**2. New Zealand Rugby Union official site**  *Web address*: www.nzrugby.com

*Content*: This site mainly focuses on the All Blacks, Super 12 and the National Provincial Championship (NPC) as well as covering the history of the game in New Zealand. It has fixtures and results, teams and players, rules of the game, tickets and travel, and there is an online shop.

The best part of the site is the 'Fanzone', which includes scheduled online chats with players (transcripts of former chats are also available on the site and provide a great insight into the personalities), discussion groups, forums, screensavers, photo galleries and the means to subscribe to an online newsletter. Users can also e-mail messages of support to the All Blacks; these messages are then posted on the site. *Rating*: 8/10

*BELOW* The Fanzone page of the New Zealand Rugby Union site.

*Dynamic content*: Updated All Black, Super 12 and NPC news articles (and comprehensive archives). The media centre is also dynamic, with press releases, press conference details and audio clips. *Rating*: 4/10

*Multimedia*: Audio clips only. *Rating*: 3/10

*Final comment*: This site is functional and easy to navigate. The fact that the fans can communicate with their heroes by chat and e-mail is the most impressive part. Live scores and video content would enhance the site.

NEW ZEALAND
**RUGBY UNION**

- NEWS
- FIXTURES | RESULTS
- HISTORY
- FANZONE

Discussion Group
Newsletter
Chat
Email the Sevens
Screensaver
Wallpaper
Player & Fan/Week
Hot Shots
All Blacks FanZone

TEAMS & PLAYERS
MEDIA CENTRE
STORE

Laws of the Game
Tickets & Travel
Contact the NZRU
Copyright &
Disclaimer

## FANZONE

### Chat
Chat live with All Black players on-line. Get your questions ready, and fire away! MORE

### Email the Sevens
Show your support for the New Zealand Sevens team - send an email now! MORE

Telecom
NEW ZEALAND

### Discussion Group
The ultimate place to have your say about the All Blacks. Sign up and get started! MORE

### Subscribe to Newsletter
Stay up-to-date with our official newsletter, brought to you by New Zealand rugby's noisiest fan, Inky. MORE

### Hot Shots
Check out the greatest shots from All Blacks, Super 12 and NPC matches. MORE

**3. South African Rugby Union official site** *Web address*: www.sarugby.net

*Content*: The site has the standard content such as results, supporters club, player profiles and shopping. The photo gallery, interactive poll, newsletter and search mechanism are notable features. *Rating*: 5/10

*Dynamic content*: News articles and press releases, updated as appropriate. *Rating*: 2/10

*Multimedia*: The most exciting parts of this site are the video highlights of tries scored by the Springboks, available for narrowband and broadband connections. These snippets are good quality and give the site colour and life. The site could be improved by adding video of interviews with players, feature stories and live webcasts of appropriate rugby events. *Rating*: 8/10

*Final comment*: It's great to finally see video of the game on a rugby site! Taken from television broadcasts of South Africa's international match coverage the on-demand video highlights are free and a great way to keep in touch with the games if you don't see them live on TV. The pages of the site, however, are relatively slow to download.

**4. Rugby Heaven site** *Web address*: http://rugbyheaven.com

*Content*: Rugby Heaven's mission is to cover all rugby with a great depth of stories and balanced views. It is owned and operated by the f2 network and draws mainly from its flagship newspaper, *The Sydney Morning Herald*, and also includes articles from the *New Zealand Herald*. This site tends to be more controversial, with feature articles from journalists such as Greg Growden and Wynne Gray. It includes information on the Tri-Nations and Super 12, news from off the field and a calendar. Users can sign up for a weekly newsletter or participate in online forums. *Rating*: 8/10

*Dynamic content*: News articles updated once a day. *Rating*: 4/10

*Multimedia*: As Rugby Heaven has no rights to match vision, they do well to include audio and video interviews with players and coaches. *Rating*: 5/10

*Final comment*: This site is heavily news based but is easy for a fan of the game to check daily and keep up with southern hemisphere (and international) rugby. Very user-friendly.

**5. Eero Tarik's rugby site**
*Web address*: www.tarik.com.au

*Content*: Super 12, Tri-Nations and World Cup. If you want live scoring or are statistics mad this is the site for you! It has a comprehensive library of statistics for current and past SANZAR matches. A great place to settle a bet with a mate. *Rating*: 4/10

*Dynamic content*: Scoring and updates live for all key matches played in the southern hemisphere. *Rating*: 7/10

*Multimedia*: None. *Rating*: 0/10

*Final comment*: Not a bad site considering one devoted fan updates it all by himself – no matter what time of the day or night the game is being played. Well done Eero Tarik!

### SUPER 12 BOOKMARKS

*If you follow a specific team or are looking for more detailed updates on the Super 12, try logging on to the official team sites:*

NSW Waratahs: www.nswrugby.com.au
ACT Brumbies: www.brumbies.com.au
QLD Reds: www.qru.com.au
Canterbury Crusaders: www.crfu.co.nz
Wellington Hurricanes: www.hurricanes.co.nz
Waikato Chiefs: www.chiefs.co.nz
Otago Highlanders: http://highlanders-rugby.com/
Auckland Blues: www.aucklandrugby.co.nz
Stormers: www.thestormers.com/
Bulls: www.thebulls.co.za
Sharks: www.sharksrugby.co.za
Cats: www.catsrugby.co.za

# Tempora Mutantur Nos et Mutamur in Illis

## by PAUL STEPHENS

'Where once we all marvelled at the tribalism and the unpredictability of the oldest international series in the calendar, there are now very real concerns for its survival. Frankly, in its present form, the tournament is threatened by rapidly diminishing appeal. If we want things to stay as they are, things will have to change. But how?'

Preserving the illusion that things will stay as they are for ever, and that nothing needs to be changed, is a game the British have played with consummate ease for generations. How else would we explain the neglect and decay of our rail and water-provision networks in the 50 years or so before privatisation? Complacency is the answer which first comes to mind.

But it wasn't always so. When the Victorians were still building an empire, the future Tory prime minister Benjamin Disraeli said during a famous 1867 speech in Edinburgh: 'Change is inevitable in a progressive country. Change is constant.' Quite so. Though it is the timing of change which is crucial, and the way we adapt to it which is the prime measurement of progress.

By the end of the most exhausting domestic rugby season in history, the two most meaningful decisions to change were made by the television broadcaster BSkyB and the game's most venerated commentator, Bill McLaren. Their timing couldn't have been more acute. In a collapsing sports rights market, with ITV Digital in free fall, BSkyB decided not to renew their interest in televising the Six Nations Championship, preferring instead to concentrate on England's autumn internationals. This left the way open for the BBC to bid for the Six Nations, which they secured with a deal which fell some way short of the £100 million asking price, the tournament's administrators having to accept an agreement which will bring in around £65 million over the next three years.

While the sigh of relief was audible throughout the game, especially from those without satellite receivers, this was followed by the disappointing news that Lloyds TSB were not renewing their option after five years as the title sponsors. With all the Twickenham games to be shown on terrestrial television, this will increase the audience viewing figures to make it – in theory at least – a more attractive proposition to a would-be sponsor. However, the new backer will be mindful that with the format changed, and matches played on seven weekends rather than ten, there will be an airtime reduction of 30 per cent. So whoever takes over from Lloyds TSB is unlikely to be persuaded to shell out the £35 million the banking firm did, for as well as the downturn in the market, the Six Nations Championship is no longer the competition it once was and, in its present form, is unlikely to be so again.

Having done so much to help popularise the tournament with his knowledgeable and at times unforgettably whimsical commentaries, Bill McLaren was the unchallenged voice of rugby. A delightful man, McLaren would not have wished to sully his untarnished reputation by declaring that his decision to retire when he did was influenced by his disappointment at the way the tournament had declined, with the Celtic countries no longer able to offer a proper challenge to England and France. But that's how it is, and last season only Scotland made England work harder than usual for victory. It was easy against Ireland and embarrassingly so against Wales, after which the England team looked as if they hardly needed a shower.

Not that we should be surprised. The warning signs were posted long ago, despite England's away defeats by Wales in 1999, the Scots a year later, and the loss to Ireland in the postponed Lansdowne Road clash last October, which meant that England had blown three Grand Slam chances on the trot. While that brought much joy to the Celts, England have established a trend against their oldest foes which shows no sign of being reversed. Consider the facts:

By comparing the performance of England against all three Celtic countries on a like-for-like basis over two periods, we can see how the red-rose brigade have become all-dominant. The brief epochs in question were the decade 1980-1989, followed by the 13 seasons from 1990 to 2002.

### England v Ireland

*1980-1989*: England won seven; England's winning margin was 11.8 points per game; Ireland won four (there was a non-championship match in 1989 which has been included).
*1990-2002*: England won ten; England's winning margin increased to 22.2 points per game; Ireland won three.

### England v Scotland

*1980-1989*: England won five; England's winning margin was 8.6 points per game; Scotland won three; there were two draws.
*1990-2002*: England won 12; England's winning margin increased to 14.75 points per game; Scotland won two (there was a World Cup game in 1991, which has been included).

### England v Wales

*1980-1989*: England won three; England's winning margin was 8.0 points per game; Wales won seven; there was one draw (there was a World Cup game in 1987, which has been included).
*1990-2002*: England won 11; England's winning margin increased to 23.2 points per game; Wales won two.

If we take a look at the differences between the periods and express them another way, we see that from 1980-1989 England's ratio of wins to losses was 15-14 – not much better than evens. In the seasons 1990-2002 the ratio was 33-7 – almost 5-1. Moreover, if we take the first years of the professional era, from 1995 to 2002, during which a total of 24 matches has been played, the ratio has improved to 7-1, there being only three defeats against 21 victories. England's winning margin has been 22.4 points per game. In that time none of the Celtic nations have won at Twickenham.

The Celts have fared little better against France. Between 1980 and 2002 France have beaten Ireland 20 times. Ireland's tally of wins is just three, with a sequence between 1983 and 1999 producing not a single victory for the men in green. Against Wales the score is 19-7 to France, which includes a run of 12 successive wins for Les Bleus since 1983. The Scots, to be fair to them, have done rather better, notching ten wins against 14 losses, though they have won only twice in Paris since 1969.

By improving the win/loss ratio – and extending their winning margins – England have not only authenticated a trend but advanced it, so that the Six Nations will increasingly be seen as a contest between France and England, with the Celtic nations having to be satisfied with an occasional victory whenever either of the big two take their eye off the ball or fail to prepare properly.

The bare statistics, telling as they are, do not provide the only indicator that all is not well with the old tournament. There has always been a strong social element to international rugby in midwinter. The trips to Edinburgh, Dublin, Paris and Cardiff – to which Rome has been added recently – are enjoyable enough in their own right. And while the BBC were televising the competition, at a time when there was very little sporting action of note going on elsewhere in Europe, the championship appeared invulnerable. Not any more, even if the return of the BBC as sole broadcaster arrests the discernible slackening of interest, at least for a season or two.

There are other factors at work – quality and quantity being but two. In Scotland and Wales there is insufficient top-grade rugby being played; and how it shows. The Welsh/Scottish League was hopelessly ineffectual as a means of preparing players for higher-class rugby and has now been abandoned, while in last season's Celtic League only Neath and Glasgow of the non-Irish teams got as high as third in their respective pools.

It was a similarly depressing story in the Heineken Cup. In seven years of this competition, neither of the Scottish clubs have ever made it to the quarter-finals. An English team has contested every final except those of 1996 and 1999, when no clubs from England participated in the competition. Four of the last five finals have been won by an English side. From Wales, just Cardiff and Pontypridd have made it to a European final. Until the Sardis Road side reached last spring's Kassam Stadium decider, only to be defeated by Sale, it seemed as if the Welsh clubs weren't interested in the shield, so is it any wonder that the game in the Principality has regressed? Or that lower standards are having a detrimental effect on the national teams of Scotland and Wales?

*BELOW* Alex Sanderson breaks Michael Owen's tackle in the Parker Pen Shield final at the Kassam Stadium, Oxford. Owen's Pontypridd – only the second Welsh club to reach a European final – were a broken side as Sale triumphed 25-22.

The situation in Ireland is somewhat different. For starters they have somehow found two or three world-class players, and their Leinster and Munster teams were better than anything to be found in Scotland or Wales. Even so, Ireland were despatched by France and England, who each won with plenty to spare, emphasising again that a real gulf in class exists between them and the Celts. Which leaves Italy, who, with a weak domestic structure, are merely making up the numbers. Unless the Italians can conjure a win or two in the next season or so, attendances for their away matches could nosedive.

With a glut of rugby on offer, the punters are becoming choosier. They want quality for their money, especially as the cost of best seats at international matches has reached the £50 mark. The quantity issue is a problem for the individual Unions, who show no signs of scaling down the calls on top players, despite making all sorts of noises to suggest they are determined to do so. Player burn-out is no longer a figment of the imagination, it is a reality.

# is **Your** Cash in **Safe** hands?

In a climate of increasing levels of crime against businesses, Securicor can help you to reduce the risk.

By outsourcing your cash management needs to an expert, you are demonstrating your commitment to security and the safety of your staff, whilst also enjoying potential cost benefits.

**Our portfolio of cash solutions includes:**

- Cash Transportation
- Cash Processing
- Safe Custody
- Coin Management
- ATM Management
- CashMachines*

**Simply call us today for further details on how our creative cash management solutions can start helping your business or to arrange a meeting without obligation.**

## securicor

**Securicor Cash Services Limited,**
**Sutton Park House, 15 Carshalton Road, Sutton, Surrey SM1 4LD**
**Tel: 020 8770 7000  www.securicor.com**

*Supplied by Securicor's subsidiary company Securicor Cash Machines Limited

England batsman Graham Thorpe, still in his prime, has retired from one-day international cricket, wearied by the never-ending impositions of the modern game. Three days after the end of the summer's seven Tests and extended one-day set-to, England flew to Sri Lanka for a one-day tournament. Two weeks later it was off to Australia for an Ashes series, followed by more one-dayers against the Australians and Sri Lanka. After that we reach the World Cup, to be played over nearly two months. This ends in late March, just in time to make ready for the new season in England.

Challenging though international cricket is, the 15-a-side game makes far greater physical demands, and something must be done about the seemingly interminable grind of everlasting rugby. The assumption that it is possible to support a ten-month season in England has been tested to destruction by the ludicrously overblown Zurich Championship. Enough is enough. More is not the answer. If we don't take care, the game will soon become an unemotional and meaningless tableau of exploitation. As things stand, much of it is already being packaged, promoted and offered to the public like a detergent.

One way to spice things up in Europe would be to admit the Springboks. There are signs that South Africa have become disenchanted with their SANZAR colleagues, and by joining the Six Nations, there are considerable advantages to be had from both playing and commercial perspectives. With Sydney 18 hours away from Johannesburg, and Auckland a further three hours distant, there is a jet-

*ABOVE* Keith Wood scores at Lansdowne Road where Ireland snatch victory in the rescheduled Six Nations match in October 2001, so denying England a Grand Slam for the third successive season.

lag problem for the players, who are also unenthusiastic about the prospect of meeting the same two teams each season. With substantial time-zone differences, Tri-Nations matches in New Zealand and Australia are screened in the morning in sports-mad South Africa, as they are in Great Britain, making them less attractive to advertisers. With only a one- or two-hour time difference between the Republic and Europe, there would be no jet lag for the players and greatly enhanced television opportunities with the Boks over here.

Nothing will be decided until the current SANZAR deal runs out in 2005. Before it is renegotiated, the European nations will need to consider the implications of enlarging their tournament from six to seven. First would be the small matter of accommodating another six matches in an already overcrowded programme. Then, in England's case particularly, there would be the loss of South Africa's autumn visit to Twickenham each year. No financial gain there. As a way of ensuring the Springboks' participation, we could have a two-division European International Championship, with Russia, Spain, Switzerland, Portugal, Belgium and Romania in the second tier, with one-up/one-down promotion and relegation. Taking a form line through the existing Six Nations Championship, were this to be the agreed revised format, Italy would be relegated in year one, before bouncing straight back up again, leaving either Wales or Scotland to drop down.

I'm dreaming of course. It isn't going to happen. New Zealand and Australia will move heaven and earth to keep South Africa on board, probably with an enlarged share of the SANZAR TV cake, because the Boks' home matches can also reach a European audience at prime time – and maybe vote to include one of Argentina, Fiji or Samoa to make it the Quad-Nations – while Europe will be left to get on with its own tournament. Which brings us back to where we started.

If one accepts the sense of the maxim about not fixing things which aren't broken, there is quite a lot of tinkering taking place in Europe, providing the clearest possible evidence that all is not well with the

***ABOVE*** The empty seats tell their own story. Twickenham was little more than a third full for the Zurich Championship final, won by Gloucester, who defeated old rivals Bristol 28-23.

***RIGHT*** A sign of times to come? Could the Springboks desert the Tri-Nations and join an enlarged European nations tournament? Too fanciful? Not everyone thinks so.

celebrated old joust. There have been calls to move it to the summer (or at least until all the domestic competitions have been completed); it will soon take place over fewer weekends; a Friday evening slot for at least one game is on the cards; and guaranteed house-full signs are a thing of the past.

For the longest-established international in the book, the Calcutta Cup, the Scottish RFU were reduced to selling tickets on the open market last January. Even the corporate hospitality firms are feeling the pinch. The chief executive of one firm told me that his company had been left with more than 200 tickets for the England v Wales clash at Twickenham. No one is likely to shed any tears for him, but his expectations for next season's Six Nations matches have been reduced accordingly; though as another sign of changing times, sales of packages for the autumn matches against the southern hemisphere big three are showing a healthy increase.

Where once we all marvelled at the tribalism and the unpredictability of the oldest international series in the calendar, there are now very real concerns for its survival. Frankly, in its present form, the tournament is threatened by rapidly diminishing appeal. If we want things to stay as they are, things will have to change. But how?

Finding a way of dealing with too much rugby should be comparatively easy. Making the changes necessary for the Six Nations Championship to prosper is altogether a trickier call. By admitting Italy in 2000 the competition has become progressively more predictable. In seeking the way ahead, those charged with the governance of the game in Europe need to be reminded of the Welshman John Owen's 17th-century dictum: *Tempora mutantur nos et mutamur in illis*. Times change and we change with them.

# SCOTTISH COURAGE
## — LIMITED —
BREWERS SINCE 1749

As the UK's leading brewer,
Scottish Courage
is proud to support the work of the
Wooden Spoon Society
in all that it has achieved.

Our best wishes for the year ahead
and may the great work continue.

# Bill McLaren
# the Voice of Rugby

## by NORMAN MAIR

'He is well aware that the commentator has not been born who does not annoy someone, but he makes no apology for having explained what was happening to the uninitiated. It might have irritated some of the cognoscenti, but, as Princess Anne put it, many of her generation owed almost everything they knew about rugby to McLaren's commentaries.'

'Heaven help the chap who has to follow him' was the reaction of the legendary Ireland and Lions international Mike Gibson to the news that Bill McLaren was to retire. 'To so many of us Bill McLaren was rugby football,' said Gareth Edwards. 'He was never critical,' noted Fran Cotton, 'but he had the respect of the players because of his knowledge of the game, his professionalism.' 'As a man and as a broadcaster, he was universally well liked,' opined Andy Irvine. 'I doubt if any administrator or player did more to popularise the game.'

**LEFT** The sincerest form of flattery ... Fans wear Bill McLaren masks on the occasion of his final match commentary, Wales v Scotland, Cardiff 2002.

**RIGHT** The face behind the voice ... On the big screen at Cardiff before that last game.

**PREVIOUS PAGE** In the box at Murrayfield before his last broadcast from Scottish HQ, Scotland v France 2002.

In the wake of his retirement, Bill McLaren now has what the family call a 'Trophy Room' – an innovation necessitated by the blizzard of testimonial gifts and mementos he accumulated as a miscellany of bodies marked his farewell season with myriad presentations. They came from organisations as diverse as the Six Nations Championship Committee and the South Wales Police, the Melrose Sevens and the *Western Mail*. The gesture from Wales's national newspaper was especially apposite, bearing in mind the banners hoisted over the years at matches in Cardiff proclaiming 'Bill McLaren; Simply the Best' or, the ultimate accolade in those parts, 'Bill McLaren is a Welshman'. He even received two beautifully mounted whistles from the referees. All right, he might not be quite the first rugby commentator to be richly appreciated by the men with the whistle, but the suspicion has to be that he is the first Border flanker to be, as it were, on their wavelength.

An MBE and an OBE, he is, of course, also the only non-player – if you can apply such a term to a Hawick and South of Scotland Scottish trialist – to be inducted into rugby's Hall of Fame. Moreover, he had already, some seasons previously, become the first man to receive the Freedom of Murrayfield, an honour which remains unique and which was rendered all the more memorable by the fact that it was formally conferred on him in front of a packed Murrayfield by Princess Anne.

The SRU were among those who gave him a painting of their home ground, with McLaren in characteristic guise at the microphone. A still more signal honour, though, was the naming of the media facilities at Murrayfield 'The Bill McLaren Press Gallery'. All of which touched him greatly, though no more than the 500-strong crowd which gathered, spontaneously, on the pitch at the Greenyards at the conclusion of the Melrose Sevens to clap him as, for the last time as the reigning BBC rugby commentator, he came down the ladder from the TV eyrie.

It is, of course, many moons since they named a street after him in his native Hawick – to wit, McLaren Court – while he takes much pride in a charming painting by the former Hawick and Scotland wing forward Adam Robson, which was presented to him by a suitably grateful Hawick RFC. Robson's painting is of Wilton Lodge Park where, in his capacity as an itinerant school PE teacher, McLaren coached generations of future Greens.

The presentation was made by another of Hawick's best-loved sons, Jim Renwick. In a story McLaren tells against himself, the master of ceremonies had evidently observed that he did not imagine that Renwick would have won 52 caps but for the tutelage of Bill McLaren. 'No, I wouldn't,' agreed Renwick, 'I'd have won 82!' – the delayed punchline as nicely timed as any scoring pass.

As retirement neared, *The Times* invited McLaren to pick his best XV from his years at the microphone, a project culminating in a dinner for the chosen at the Grosvenor House Hotel. The least controversial of television pundits proceeded to stir up the proverbial hornet's nest by picking nine of his XV from the northern hemisphere and by omitting such as Michael Jones, John Eales, J.P.R. Williams and both Barry John and Phil Bennett, not to mention Jonah Lomu of the 1995 World Cup. 'They may not have been the best 15 players I ever saw,' shrugs McLaren, 'but they were the 15 players who, for a variety of reasons, had most appealed to me as a television commentator.'

The BBC in Scotland paid their own tribute with an eminently watchable documentary entitled simply *The Voice*. John Beattie was at his best as narrator-cum-interviewer, while the producer and director was one of McLaren's past primary school pupils, Grigor Sterling. It was at Monte Cassino in Italy that McLaren had seen action in World War II, and one of the many admirable touches were shots of McLaren revisiting the scene of that often blood-curdling battle. McLaren had come out of the army as an acting captain, and it had been the Royal Artillery who translated him from a midfield back good enough to have played for the South Schools into a flank forward standing 6ft 1in and weighing 14st 7lbs.

McLaren was still only 23 when he was struck down by tuberculosis. It is a reminder of how times have changed that the attentive Bette, the mannequin who was destined to become his wife, would take him 100 cigarettes a week which he would surreptitiously smoke under the cover of bedclothes. The initial estimate was that he would be flat on his back for four years, but he was one of the patients selected as a glorified guinea pig for the new drug streptomycin. McLaren, who was out of hospital in little more than 18 months, has no doubt that streptomycin saved his life, though it could not save his rugby career.

He is well aware that the commentator has not been born who does not annoy someone, but he makes no apology for having explained what was happening to the uninitiated. It might have

irritated some of the cognoscenti, but, as Princess Anne put it, many of her generation owed almost everything they knew about rugby to McLaren's commentaries. He gave the viewer confidence, she suggested, having given the matter some deep thought; made him or or her feel that they were privy even to some of the game's least obvious subtleties.

The so-called Big Sheets which McLaren was wont to compile before internationals, in a variety of colours and containing almost all the information he could possibly require, have become among the most coveted of rugby's latter day artefacts. Such a sheet has been known to fetch as much as £8000 at a charity auction, while no present he received on his 50th birthday tickled Andy Irvine more than the Big Sheet from 16 December 1972, the day he made his Scotland debut versus Ian Kirkpatrick's All Blacks.

In his heyday, McLaren was marvellously well versed in the letter of the laws, while his identification of players was superb. Much of it was down to his religious attendance at the teams' pre-match training sessions, but it also owed much to a trick of the trade he had picked up from the horse-racing commentaries of Raymond Glendenning.

# Very front row.

**Strong** Performance. **Solid** Delivery. **Disciplined** Investment Process.

Individual Savings Accounts (ISAs), PEP transfers, Pensions and Savings Plans, Investment Trusts and Open Ended Funds, Private Client Portfolio Management, Institutional Fund Management.

Edinburgh Fund Managers is one of the largest independent fund management groups in the UK.

**Edinburgh**
**FUND MANAGERS**

ROCK **SOLID**

Regulated by the Financial Services Authority.

Glendenning, he read, had a pack of cards, each depicting the racing colours of an owner. He would shuffle the cards until identification was automatic. McLaren adapted the practice to his own pre-match preparation, using a pack of ordinary playing cards suitably doctored to represent a rugby team. Before an international, he would flick through the cards until he could instantly match the player to the number. It was a device which had worked supremely well for him until he was momentarily thrown by the fact that the Scotland centre James McLaren had shed the '3' from his number 13 jersey, leaving a totally misleading figure '1' on his back. That was bad enough, but at least it was an isolated incident. Much more of an occupational hazard has been the spread, even among the backs, of the scrum cap, an item of headgear which, of course, tends to make all those using the same make look horribly alike.

Famously unbiased, McLaren had a broadcasting voice, born of the Scottish Borders, which was unlikely to give offence at either end of the social spectrum. There was warmth in that voice and, at the right moments, an irresistibly infectious excitement. Though his father had hailed from the West, McLaren himself is a Borderer through and through, delighting in the local rivalries and the humour. His grandson, Rory Lawson, son of Alan Lawson of Scotland fame, found himself in his more youthful schooldays playing against a school team which featured the offspring of a former Border flanker, a notably good but abrasive player who, notoriously, had never been exactly angelic in the use he made of his feet. Soon, that worthy's lad came round the scrum and visited upon the person of Bill's grandson an unruly foot. 'That was a bit unnecessary,' protested McLaren, or words to that effect. 'I'm sorry, Bill,' said the erstwhile flanker, shaking his head sadly. 'I'm afraid he gets it from his mother ...'

There was, too, the time when Gala had in their ranks, at least for those days, an unusually large number of players from outside the town. When they arrived at Mansfield Park, they found that Hawick had in their side a former Gala player in Colin Gass. 'I see,' remarked one Gala supporter to a Hawick acquaintance, 'that you've got a Gala man in your team.' 'I see,' retorted the other, who recognised an open goal when it beckoned, 'that you've got one too.' Bill loved that.

**ABOVE** Signing off at the Millennium Stadium. To quote Fran Cotton, Bill McLaren 'was never critical, but he had the respect of the players because of his knowledge of the game, his professionalism.'

# Work, Rest and Play
## England's World Cup Build-up
### by MICK CLEARY

'The sensible management of players is the key issue facing the game. The northern hemisphere season is too long. Everyone says so. Everyone acknowledges as much. And yet nobody does a damn thing about it. Everyone wants their slice of the pie – even the players.'

To rest or play? That is the question. England have gone for hard labour, with 13 Tests between the start of the 2002-03 season and the beginning of the Rugby World Cup in early October 2003. It's a heavy load but one Clive Woodward insists is the right way to gear up for the most significant event in the rugby calendar.

Woodward is desperate not to repeat the failings of the last tournament, when England went down meekly to the Springboks on a dismal Sunday afternoon in Paris. That quarter-final defeat left its mark. It almost cost Woodward his job as questions were asked, and rightly so. Woodward survived, and rightly so. He has invested a lot of time, effort, brain cells and RFU money into not repeating the mistakes this time around.

England's principal blemish was perceived to be a lack of meaningful preparation. They had warm-up games but against the second tier of rugby nations – Canada and the USA – before a final hit-out against a scratch Premiership XV. The schedule was useful but not unduly taxing. This time around England will play France home and away and Wales at the Millennium Stadium in Cardiff. Those games take place in August. Rugby World Cup has always insisted that the month before a tournament be kept clear of international rugby to avoid undermining the event itself. The England players will then have a clear five-week run-in to the World Cup itself. Some will play for their clubs; some will not.

Once again the fine line between work and rest will have to be carefully calibrated. Remember that the domestic season itself will not have finished until 7 June, over eight months after it began – a ludicrous state of affairs. Then England pack their bags and head south to play Test matches in Australia and New Zealand. That trip will be no picnic as both sides look to score psychological one-upmanship points before the real thing. Add to that schedule three autumn Tests and five outings in the Six Nations.

It will be hard yakka. However, England are woefully lacking in competitive match practice on the road. Bring a team to Twickenham – and the big three, New Zealand, Australia and South Africa, are all due in November 2002 – and England take on all-comers with confidence. Once the Twickenham comfort zone is in the rear-view mirror, though, that sense of invincibility vanishes. England's last defeat at HQ came during the 1999 World Cup, the All Blacks beating them 30-16 in a pool game. (Some bloke by the name of Lomu did some damage – and not for the first time in a World Cup match against England.) Yet England have lost to Wales, Scotland and Ireland on alien turf in recent years – albeit Wembley, where Wales denied England the Grand Slam in 1999, is but a few miles along London's North Circular from Twickenham. England have also gone down to South Africa in Pretoria (somewhat unluckily), to Australia in Sydney and to France in Paris.

*ABOVE RIGHT* The end of the road in 1999. England captain Martin Johnson leaves the field after the 44-21 Paris defeat by the Boks in the quarter-finals of the last World Cup.

*RIGHT* England's current form at HQ is excellent. Dan Luger and Will Greenwood celebrate the former's try to seal the 29-9 victory over South Africa in November 2001.

They need to find out more about themselves – as to why on earth a change in surroundings should seemingly make a difference. The pitch is the same, the opposition familiar, so why the problem? The southern hemisphere players are better versed in toughing it out against an inhospitable backdrop. All their Super 12 men spend significant time on the road, heading across oceans, combating fatigue and hostile crowds to do battle. The England players have at least started to get up to speed on that front in recent years through their Heineken Cup experiences. There are few more intimidating places to do your stuff than in the deep south of France. Perpignan's Stade Aime Giral, with its fenced-in crowd and firecrackers, is not for the faint-hearted.

So Woodward has opted to forge his men in the toughest possible circumstances. It's a brave call. The recent football World Cup showed up the benefits of rest over work. The heavily fancied teams, such as France and Argentina, along with the likes of Italy and Portugal, all wilted. So too England. All their players looked drained after the rigours of a domestic and Champions League season. Those that prospered, and unexpectedly so, like South Korea and the USA, had fitter and fresher players at their disposal.

Woodward argues that his players have had their down time, 20 or so of them missing the brief flit to Argentina in the summer of 2002 for a one-off Test against the Pumas. The side that did so well to beat Argentina 26-18 at Velez Sarsfield – only seven days after the Pumas

**ABOVE** Jonny Wilkinson was one of many senior players who did not take part in England's trip to Argentina in summer 2002. Indeed the tour party contained only four international regulars.

**RIGHT** Clive Woodward believes that more time with his players is key to England's fortunes in the coming World Cup.

had seen off Grand Slam champions, France – contained only four England regulars. The likes of Martin Johnson, Jonny Wilkinson, Neil Back, Kyran Bracken and many others were taking time out – not to chill and pig out like we mere mortals might do but to get stuck in to some serious preseason training. Of course they also needed to unwind and recharge, but the principal benefit for these guys would be the opportunity to hit some heavy-duty weights in the gym and build the stamina base. Any Olympic athlete will tell you that off-season training is far more important than any training done during the season itself. And Neil Back will support every word of that view. He may not recommend the means of going about it – a six-month ban for pushing referee Steve Lander at the end of the 1996 Pilkington Cup final – but he would wholly endorse the outcome. Back's long lay-off enabled him to bulk up, to become stronger and fitter. So too for Woodward's men in summer 2002.

At least that is how the theory goes. It will be proven one way or another only after the event. The sensible management of players is the key issue facing the game. The northern hemisphere season is too long. Everyone says so. Everyone acknowledges as much. And yet nobody does a damn thing about it. Everyone wants their slice of the pie – even the players. Not one of them has offered to take a pay cut in return for, say, half a dozen games being knocked off the fixture list. What happens too when the Barbarians come calling – good cause, good crack and a few quid? Sign here, please. There is a lunge for the dotted line all around the world.

The International Board is also culpable. The autumn schedule is already gruelling, with Test matches back to back throughout Europe. And yet the board have seen fit to organise a northern versus southern hemisphere match. Again the cause is good – raising funds to support the ailing countries – but the message is all wrong. Someone has to take a stand. Someone has to say to hell with the cash flow. Quality not quantity is what the game is crying out for. Less can so often be more.

Woodward fully intends to mix and match his squad of players throughout the international season. He wants to give the likes of Charlie Hodgson proper game time so that if Jonny Wilkinson were to be crocked in the early stages of the 2003 World Cup then the Sale fly half would be properly prepared to step in. Hodgson will not be the only one to get a run as Woodward rotates the main men, resting them, preparing the others and also putting everyone on their toes.

Woodward has also fought ferociously to secure more contact time with his players. He saw them only twice outside the normal release time for internationals during the 2001-02 season. He has requested far more contact with them – 18 slots throughout the season. Woodward insists that if he does not have this time then England's campaign in the World Cup will be based on hope rather than expectation. The England set-up is now one of the most thorough and professional in the world, underpinned by state-of-the-art computer technology. If that sort of million-pound investment is to pay off, then Woodward needs more access.

That relationship, between club and country, is the key to English hopes for the 2003 World Cup. If it all comes to fruition, then England are in with a real chance of lifting the William Webb Ellis Trophy. If it doesn't, if there are constant arguments and stand-offs, then keep your money in your wallet.

The build-up to the 2003 World Cup, the jockeying for favouritism, the subtle swings in fortunes, the late emergence of unexpected stars (remember Lomu's thunderous and unheralded entrance in 1995) and the feverish chase for tickets (expect another Lions-type invasion from these parts) will ensure a fascinating few months.

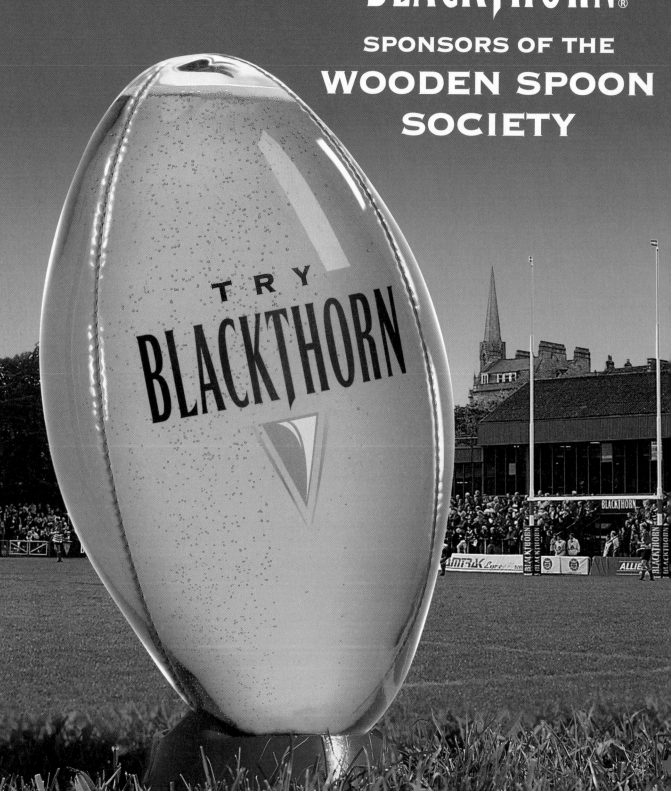

# CLUBS WORLDWIDE

# Three-time Tigers?
# Stand by for Euro action

### by STEPHEN JONES

'Leicester's group last season was reasonably comfortable, and with the greatest possible respect to the teams involved, you have to say that it is unlikely that Leicester's pool-mates for 2002-03 – Neath, Béziers and Calvisano – will stop them.'

In the fields of sport and commerce it is always priceless when you have on your hands a guaranteed success, and rugby's marketing and commercial people, not to mention television companies and the general rugby-watching public, will therefore spend much of the new season in gleeful anticipation of the Heineken European Cup, not to mention an ugly duckling now assuming the most glossy feathers – the Parker Pen Shield.

On the grounds that we do not want results to become too predictable there is a slight jar to optimism when you consider the attempt of Leicester Tigers to achieve a stunning hat-trick when the new European season begins. One of the great benefits in winning the event is that you are seeded top for the next year and have an easier group. Leicester's group last season was reasonably comfortable, and with the greatest possible respect to the teams involved, you have to say that it is unlikely that Leicester's pool-mates for 2002-03 – Neath, Béziers and Calvisano – will stop them.

It is one of the unwritten rules of European competition that teams taking part for the first time and teams who have missed some years of the event need at least two seasons to attune themselves to what is a standard of rugby dramatically higher than they are used to on the domestic scene. In terms of intensity and class, the latter stages of the Heineken Cup compared more than favourably with international rugby. It is doubtful if even the fervent Welshmen at Neath or the former giants of Béziers will have enough Euro experience.

Before discussing the forthcoming pools it is important to put a dead stop to one theory doing the rounds which constitutes the only danger to the future prosperity of the England club game – the theory that more and more teams should be added to the Heineken event, and that it should become a European league. This is dangerous nonsense and not only on the basis that the expansion of the European Cup in football has diminished its own appeal by adding teams. It is, perhaps, understandable in this greedy age in rugby that more teams should wish to enter the event. But to increase the competitors beyond the current number (24) and to achieve the abomination of making the whole thing a boring league would be to forget entirely the point of it. The Heineken Cup is an elite event for the cream of the sport in the major

European rugby nations. It galvanises the previous domestic season out of sight as teams try to reach that elite, but to introduce teams who have enjoyed only a mediocre domestic season is to lose credibility. I was delighted to hear Derek McGrath, chief executive of European Rugby Cup (ERC), proclaiming his view that the event will remain an elite tournament and that the closing stages will always be knockout in format. Quite right too.

It is also time to pay tribute to McGrath and to ERC. When that body was first formed it contained too many old codgers who had come up through the amateur ranks and had fought hard to stop professionalism arriving. Nowadays, the modern era has dawned and the body comprises chiefly new-style administrators. Where McGrath scored magnificently was in his wholly successful attempts to clean up rugby's touch lines.

Rugby had become incredibly scruffy as horde after horde of people gradually made it their business to wander up and down the touch lines and spill out of the training dugouts. If you added up the ridiculous number of replacements the game now allows, about ten medical personnel, various other posers with earpieces, a raft of media people, water carriers and other extras, it often seemed that there were more people on the touch lines than on the terraces.

This makes the whole appearance of a rugby field look littered and scruffy; it hides advertising signs, it blocks the view of spectators. These days, proud grounds such as Kingsholm look like something the cat dragged in, so many and so scruffy are the people parading up and down. McGrath has seen enough, and ERC has drastically restricted the numbers allowed on the touch line; because of this, European games are now far more attractive than the domestic and international matches in any country.

There is a change in the Parker Pen Shield, too. The event has been only a partial success over the years, at least partly because of the miserable lack of vision of French and English rugby clubs in their attitude to taking part. The French clubs have been appalling, and the situation reached its nadir when Agen went to Ebbw Vale last season and treated the whole game as a joke, deliberately conceding try after try. Nothing I can think of so violates the whole ethos of the game.

I must confess that I became Agen's most fervent supporter after that. I wanted them to do well enough in the domestic French competition to qualify for next season in the Heineken Cup itself. They have been banned from European competition and I wanted them to hurt. They did do well, they qualified and they will now miss out, and miss out also on over £1 million. It serves them right. I would have banned them for 20 years.

*ABOVE* For the second year running, Austin Healey helps to turn the Heineken Cup final. Here he breaks Ronan O'Gara's tackle and goes on to score Leicester's second try in their 15-9 victory over Munster in the 2001-02 final at the Millennium Stadium.

*RIGHT* Leicester exult at the final whistle in Cardiff, while Munster sink to their knees in despair. Can the Irishmen bounce back after two Heineken final defeats in three seasons?

*PREVIOUS PAGES* Two-time winners Leicester break out the fizz in Cardiff.

The other irony was that they missed a superb event, culminating in a dramatic win for Sale over a fine Pontypridd team in the final in Oxford. This time around, instead of a league format, teams will play home and away and the aggregate scores will give them passage on a knockout basis. It is a brave try which deserves to succeed, and with the likes of Bath in the event it will be classy too.

The big stuff will be bigger than ever. Pool A may well prove to be a canter for Leicester, although when they travel to the Gnoll it could well be that the team and the crowd in that tiny stadium recall the grand old days. Pool B is more competitive, with Viadana up against it in taking on Gloucester, Perpignan and Munster. I think it will be hard for Munster to raise themselves again, having come so close to glory of late. Both Gloucester and Perpignan are potentially brilliant, but both will need to demonstrate that they can win away. The Catalan fervour when Perpignan entertain Gloucester will be sensational.

Llanelli will hope to maintain their proud run in Europe in Pool C, when they line up against Sale, Bourgoin and Glasgow. Llanelli will be favourites, but it is just conceivable that their lapses away from home will give Sale a sniff. Sale are new to the event and will have to improve massively, but they are clever, quick and good.

In Pool D, Leinster have a chance to emulate Munster as thorn in the side of Europe, and Montferrand, Swansea and Bristol will have to find another 20 points on their domestic form last year to hold them. Pool E is arguably the toughest, with Toulouse and Newport due to do battle again, the improving Edinburgh a challenge at last and London Irish added as a powerful new element. Cardiff, Northampton and Ulster are old adversaries in Europe, and in Pool F, which pits them with Biarritz, it could be that one away victory would do the job.

But as I say, entertainment and tension and packed houses are guaranteed. Provided no one tinkers with the magic chemistry, then it will once again be proven that international rugby is not the whole story. Two major competitions to come. The chase for Leicester's crown is on.

# Sharks Sign In
## the Parker Pen Shield final 2002
### by CHRIS HEWETT

'Unfortunately for them, the Sale that emerged from the half-time rollicking dished out by their custodians – Jim Mallinder and Steve Diamond – was entirely different from the one that fired blanks throughout the opening period.'

A quiet spring Sunday amid the dreaming spires? Not quite. Not at all, actually. There was enough noise in Oxford on the last weekend in May to raise the dead from their resting places, distract the aesthetes from their poetry and waken the hearties from their beer-soaked slumbers. The European rugby show was in town for the second time in a month, and the locals caught the full blast once again. The best part of 12,000 spectators congregated at the Kassam Stadium – a record crowd for the venue – and helped the Parker Pen Shield come of age in a chorus of song and a kaleidoscope of colour.

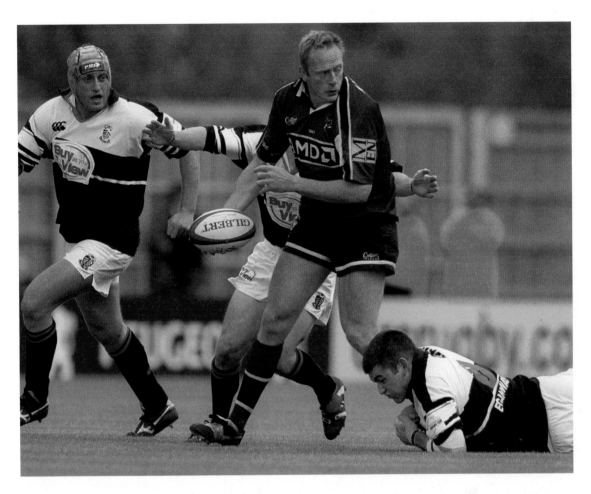

The tournament deserved its 80 minutes in the sun; indeed, it is fair to suggest that no tournament was ever more deserving of an even break. There had been scandal and sharp practice during the pool stages, when the French clubs who had dominated the competition for the first four years of its existence decided the franc was no longer worth the candle. Bourgoin, for instance, failed to register a number of leading players in an attempt to maximise their chances in the French domestic championship. When the powerful Agen club, committed to a similar prioritisation, deliberately lost their final pool match at Ebbw Vale, the stench was overwhelming. Agen were subsequently suspended from all European rugby for a year, and quite right too.

But would it be possible for the shield, in its first season with a title sponsor, to thrive without a wholehearted commitment from France? The answer to that one was never really in doubt. There were too many mismatches in the early stages, although the two Spanish clubs, from Madrid and Valladolid, punched above their weight, and Viadana, who would end the season as Italian champions, took great delight in undermining the ambitions of their elders and supposed betters. But once the competition moved into the knockout stage, the quality burned as brightly as the ambition of those clubs chasing an automatic Heineken Cup place for 2002-03.

By the time of the final, Sale had already secured their Heineken place. In many ways, they had been the team of the season in England: Jason Robinson had built on his Lions experience and was now the most dangerous attacking full back in the world; Mark Cueto, entirely unknown at the start of term, had finished the Premiership programme at the top of the try-scoring chart; Charlie Hodgson and Bryan Redpath

*ABOVE* Sharks No. 8 Peter Anglesea attracts the attention of the Ponty forwards.

*LEFT* Sale centre Mel Deane runs at Pontypridd skipper and scrum half Paul John during the Sharks' 25-22 victory in the 2002 Parker Pen Shield final.

had established themselves as the cleverest half-back pairing around; Chris Jones, a former basketball specialist, had emerged as a ball-winning lock of serious potential; Stu Pinkerton, their preseason signing from the New South Wales Waratahs, had brought some Super 12 devil to the back row; and Pete Anglesea recovered from a traumatic disciplinary affair (he was cleared by a Rugby Football Union tribunal of the unpardonable sin of gouging during a match with Newcastle) to such effect that he earned a place on England's summer tour of Argentina.

Against them were Pontypridd, widely considered second only to Llanelli as the most dedicated European adventurers in the Principality. They had ended up outside the top five Welsh finishers in the domestic league and therefore needed to win the shield to beat Swansea to a Heineken spot. Like Sale, they had introduced a raft of bright new players to the mix, and five of their pack – Mefin Davies, the excellent Wales A hooker; Gethin Jenkins, a highly rated young loose-head prop; Robert Sidoli, their ball-winning lock; Richard Parks, a real pirate of an open-side flanker; and Michael Owen, a No. 8 with footballing skills that live up to his name – had played themselves into the Wales squad for the two-Test visit to South Africa. A classic confrontation in prospect, then: Sale's state-of-the-art back division against a tough, vibrant Ponty forward unit.

**ABOVE**  Sharks right wing Steve Hanley is grabbed by Pontypridd centre Sonny Parker. Hanley was one of three Sharks try scorers along with centres Martin Shaw and Dan Harris.

**RIGHT**  Sale former full back turned coach Jim Mallinder and captain Bryan Redpath get their hands on the Parker Pen Shield.

**FOLLOWING PAGES**  The victorious Sale Sharks.

And so it unfolded. Driven along by Parks, whose banditry knew no bounds, the Ponty pack squeezed Sale at the set pieces and earned the dangerous Brett Davey a series of kicks at goal. Davey did not disappoint, landing four penalties in a highly competitive first half. Ceri Sweeney, a less assured figure than Davey but alive to whatever scoring opportunity might come his way, added a smart dropped goal, and with the English side restricted to a single Hodgson penalty, Ponty went into the interval 15-3 to the good and set fair for glory.

Unfortunately for them, the Sale that emerged from the half-time rollicking dished out by their custodians – Jim Mallinder and Steve Diamond – was entirely different from the one that fired blanks throughout the opening period. Jones, their elastically athletic lock, was the first to set about putting the world to rights; he pilfered Ponty ball at consecutive line outs to take his side to within sight of the opposition line, and then won clean ball on his own throw to set in motion a decisive attack that ended with Martin Shaw crossing to the left of the posts.

Steve Hanley, capped by England in 1999 and desperate to repeat the experience, was the next to knock a gaping hole in the renowned Ponty spirit, slipping away from Gareth Wyatt and the covering Davey after some daylight robbery at scrum-time by the ever-alert Redpath. Then it was Hodgson, very much in Clive Woodward's plans for next year's World Cup, to deal the Welshmen a sickening blow to morale. The Sale forwards had struggled at the set piece for much of the proceedings, but when Redpath rescued poor ball from the heels of his retreating pack and flicked a pass to his partner, Hodgson moved from back foot to front foot in a trice, transfixed the Ponty midfield with a magical show of the ball and sent Dan Harris, a centre replacement for Mel Deane, hurtling over for the game-breaking score.

Ponty ran themselves silly in an effort to turn the tide, but their only second-half strike was a typically well-executed mauling effort from the admirable Davies. At the final whistle, they were short by three points: Sale had won 25-22, and Ponty were out of the Heineken frame. They will be back in shield contention in the autumn, though, and will want to win the tournament for its own sake. And Sale? Their season, magnificent in all facets, was made all the more special by the capture of a first major trophy. As their supporters agreed, there are worse places than Oxford to spend a May afternoon.

Powergen is proud to support all levels of English club rugby

www.powergenrugby.co.uk

POWERGEN

# Irish Strike Silver
# the 2002 Powergen Cup final

by ALASTAIR HIGNELL

'That the Irish defence, superbly marshalled by player-coach Brendan Venter, should apply a stranglehold on the Northampton attackers was hardly surprising – it had been the rock on which their outstanding Premiership season had been built. But the way a previously unheralded back line succeeded in tearing hole after hole in the Saints' defence was simply stunning.'

A new sponsor, a new standard of excellence and a new name in the record books – London Irish gained their first piece of silverware in over a century of trying with one of the outstanding performances in cup final history. Their only regret, and that of many a neutral observer, was that such a superlative performance wasn't enough on its own to earn them a place in the Heineken Cup. It can be no coincidence that next year's Powergen Cup winners will automatically qualify for a place among Europe's elite.

As it happened, both the Exiles and their cup final opponents, Northampton, got into Europe on the back of their Premiership placings. Irish ended the league season in fourth place; the Saints just a point and a place behind. They won more Premiership matches than the Exiles, but in the unforgiving eyes of Kiwi coach Wayne Smith no statistic in the world can make up for the drubbing his team received at Twickenham.

**LEFT** London Irish centre Geoff Appleford, having snaffled an interception, runs away from Northampton's Nick Beal to score his second, and the Exiles' fourth, try.

**PREVIOUS PAGE** Full back Michael Horak celebrates scoring the second London Irish try after 20 minutes.

In a 38-7 victory, the Irish racked up the third highest total in a cup final and the third highest number of tries with five. Only Bath with eight touchdowns in 48 points against Gloucester in 1990 and Saracens with seven tries in an identical total against Wasps in 1998 have been more prolific. In addition the 31-point winning margin was the second highest in the 31 years since the tournament began. Northampton, Heineken Cup winners at Twickenham two years previously, when they had also contested the national knockout cup final, had a sudden and inexplicable attack of stage fright.

A Northampton season that had plumbed the depths of despair in December looked to have been turned gloriously around under Smith. A surge up the Premiership had been matched by a series of impressive cup results, culminating in a 38-point blitz against Newcastle in the semi-finals. With London Irish only edging past Harlequins in the other semi-final – two late penalties from Barry Everitt sealing a 32-27 victory – Northampton arrived at Twickenham for a fourth final in 12 years as slight favourites.

But the Exiles, whose only previous visit to Headquarters had resulted in defeat by Leicester back in 1980, took control of the match from the start. Northampton, whose change strip made them nearly as unrecognisable as their lacklustre play, began the match on the back foot, as Everitt fluffed an early penalty and snatched at an attempted dropped goal. Save for a spell in the middle section of the match when Ben Cohen scored their only try, they never looked like achieving any real forward momentum.

That the Irish defence, superbly marshalled by player-coach Brendan Venter, should apply a stranglehold on the Northampton attackers was hardly surprising – it had been the rock on which their outstanding Premiership season had been built. But the way a previously unheralded back line succeeded in tearing hole after hole in the Saints' defence was simply stunning.

Geoff Appleford scored the first try on the quarter-hour when a great run from wing Justin Bishop set up the attacking position from which Everitt, Venter and Bishop combined to work the centre under the posts. Five minutes later, it was full back Michael Horak who sliced through the Northampton defence and who, after a couple of desperate rucks on the Saints' line, picked up to dive over from close range. When Bishop scored the Exiles' third try just before half-time, after

Appleford and Horak had carved out the opening, the game was as good as over. Everitt converted all three tries and added a penalty, and the Exiles were 24-0 ahead at the break.

Things got a little better for the Saints immediately after half-time, but not much. At least they managed to provoke the opposition into acts of indiscretion rather than themselves. While Matt Dawson and captain Budge Pountney had gone down the half-time tunnel locked in a heated argument, now Dawson attracted a head-high tackle from Venter, and Exiles prop Mike Worsley and Northampton replacement prop Robbie Morris were sent to the sin-bin for fighting. Amid the mayhem Ben Cohen scored for Northampton, leaping high to take a perfectly weighted up-and-under from Paul Grayson, who converted from wide out.

> **BELOW** No. 8 Chris Sheasby (centre), formerly of Wasps and Harlequins, shows off the Powergen Cup with Exiles player-coach Brendan Venter.

But just when it seemed that Northampton might make a game of it, Appleford intercepted a Dawson pass from deep within his own 22 to gallop away for his second try, while deep in injury time Bishop also bagged his second. Everitt converted both, and the Saints' misery was complete.

As for the Irish, joy was all but unconfined. 'It doesn't get any better than this' was the opinion of Brendan Venter, and it couldn't have been a better example of the way in which the ebullient South African has revolutionised his club, and the Premiership. In taking a handful of veterans (such as himself, lock Steve Williams and the ageless No. 8 Chris Sheasby), a clutch of hard-nosed operators from the former colonies (men like hooker Naka Drotske, captain Ryan Strudwick and scrum half Hentie Martens) and mixing them with the proven Premiership talents like Everitt and Bishop, Venter had produced a team that was far greater than its parts. In doing so, he had also brought the best out of an exciting crop of youngsters, three of whom – Appleford, Horak and flanker Declan Danaher – were to be rewarded with places on the England tour to Argentina.

In the light of their Twickenham humiliation, Northampton might not be inclined to agree, but London Irish in particular and English rugby in general owe a great deal to the good doctor from Cape Town.

# The leading force in supplying building, timber, plumbing & heating materials and tool hire.

**Travis Perkins**

# Crusaders' 4 in 5 Super 12 2002

## by RAECHELLE EDWARDS

'"The Crusaders were outstanding in all facets of the game and have taken the game to a new level and set the standard for all other teams to try to aspire to," said coach of the Brumbies, David Nucifora.'

The Canterbury Crusaders are being dubbed the greatest provincial rugby team in the world following the 2002 Super 12 competition. Such high praise is reserved only for truly magnificent sides. The Crusaders have earned it, as they have undeniably set the standard for southern hemisphere rugby. They play the game with a breathtaking combination of fast, elusive back-line play and industrious, powerful forwards that sets them apart.

Canterbury were consistent from the start of the competition, steadily chalking up victories. Rounds One to Four saw the Crusaders defeat the Otago Highlanders, Waikato Chiefs, Auckland Blues and Queensland Reds, but none of these matches were annihilations – the Crusaders were just starting to find their rhythm. They won four of their first five matches by seven points or less, two of those victories coming after goals in the dying seconds. It was this calm and professional attitude that the Crusaders upheld throughout the tournament.

After a Round Five bye, the Christchurch-based outfit faced their arch-rivals, the ACT Brumbies. The defending champions were on a roll, too. They had won five from five in typical Brumbies style – quick ball from the forwards allowing halves George Gregan and Stephen Larkham to release their swift back line.

This match was to set up a fascinating test of dominance in the southern hemisphere's premier provincial rugby competition. It was the halfway point of the tournament, Sunday 31 March, when the two teams met in Christchurch. The Brumbies snatched a 32-30 lead in the 76th minute after earlier trailing 30-18 with 20 minutes left on the clock. In a war of attrition Aaron Mauger's field goal with one minute remaining proved the difference – the Crusaders winners 33 points to 32.

It was a spectacular win instigated by the class of Crusaders five-eighth Andrew Mehrtens, who guided Canterbury to victory with five penalties, a field goal and a conversion for a personal tally of 20 points. Mehrtens' brilliant season continued as he perfected his combinations with scrum half Justin Marshall and inside centre Aaron Mauger. The number 12 jersey for the All Blacks has been

a problematic one for so many years, and an answer was now emerging in Mauger, who was the find of the tournament.

That one-point loss sparked a mini-slump for the Brumbies, who after a bye in Round Seven, went on to lose Rounds Eight, Nine and Ten, before recovering to post victories in the final two rounds. The Crusaders, on the other hand, grew in confidence, facing weak South African opponents. They comfortably beat the Bulls, Stormers, Sharks and Cats before returning to New Zealand and overcoming the Wellington Hurricanes. Round Twelve saw a defining moment in rugby – Canterbury humiliated the New South Wales Waratahs by the biggest winning margin in Super 12 history, a 96-19 demolition.

Earlier in the season the Bob Dwyer-coached Waratahs side had been touted as a tournament favourite, but the Crusaders exposed the team's lack of big-game experience. The Waratahs were unable to cope with the Crusaders' dynamic and powerful game. Canterbury humbled the New South Wales side, outscoring them 14 tries to 3. The Waratahs and the Queensland Reds had both welcomed new players to their teams in 2002, including high-profile rugby league internationals Mat Rogers and Wendell Sailor, who boosted the profile of rugby union in Australia.

The Crusaders beat the Highlanders in the semi-final and won the right to host the final. Their opponents were the ACT Brumbies, who had further humiliated the Waratahs by 41 points in their semi-final. In howling wind and rain and temperatures nudging zero degrees at Jade Stadium, Christchurch, in the South Island of New Zealand, the challenge was set. The Brumbies were playing for back-to-back title victories and the Crusaders were chasing their fourth Super 12 title in five years. Of the 30 starting players in the final, 27 had Test match experience. Fijian World Cup winger Marika Vunibaka lined up for the Crusaders with 14 All Blacks as his team-mates.

The game epitomised the Crusaders in the 2002 Super 12 – patient, efficient and ruthless. The Brumbies were being strangled out of the game, and then they lost their playmaker, Larkham, who suffered

*ABOVE* Mat Rogers attacks for the Waratahs as they go down 51-10 against the Brumbies in the semis.

*RIGHT* Crusaders lock Chris Jack on the charge during his side's 31-13 victory over the Brumbies in the final.

*PREVIOUS PAGE* Aaron Mauger scores for the Crusaders during their Round 12 96-19 demolition of the Waratahs.

ligament damage in his elbow. To their credit, the Brumbies launched a comeback and with just eight minutes remaining were suddenly only one point behind after winger Andrew Walker seized on a wayward Justin Marshall pass and ran 45 metres to score. An unruly line-out throw and another intercept saw the Crusaders reassert their dominance and literally run away with the game, capping the most impressive of unbeaten seasons.

The Crusaders had won their three previous Super 12 championships away, so this victory was even sweeter. 'Winning at home is very personal, when you know so many people in the crowd ... their friends, their family. It doesn't get a lot better than that,' said Canterbury coach Robbie Deans. 'The Crusaders were outstanding in all facets of the game and have taken the game to a new level and set the standard for all other teams to try to aspire to,' said coach of the Brumbies, David Nucifora. 'The Super 12 really does drive the direction of the game and the way it is being played,' Deans said. '[Former All Black coach] Wayne Smith commented to me once that he found it difficult not being part of the Super 12 because when the guys came together for the national team, the game would have moved on. And it does ... from the start of the Super 12 campaign to the end, methods change and what you are applying at the start may not be appropriate at the end.'

So what makes the Crusaders so successful? What inspires their ability to dominate opposing teams and make it look so easy? Firstly, they are an incredibly well-balanced side. From 1 to 15 they are solid, consistent players with total commitment. And beyond the 1st XV the depth in the squad is obvious – when they lose one player to injury another reliable player always seems to be there to fill the gap. They have no weaknesses. Opposing sides are lost when they try to fathom what to target, as there is no vulnerability, only potential human error on the field. This side has a complete passion for winning and dedication to securing the ball.

Brumbies captain Gregan says the reason his team struggled in the final was because the opposition had denied the visitors enough possession to seriously challenge. Stunning performances came from the Canterbury back row of Richard McCaw, Reuben Thorne and Scott Robertson, who were devastating at the breakdown, and lock Chris Jack made a name for himself as a future star of

**LEFT** Master stand-off Andrew Mehrtens attempts a conversion during Canterbury's 33-32 Round Six win over the Brumbies.

**RIGHT** Tournament top try scorer Roger Randle on his way to the line for the Chiefs against the Stormers at Hamilton.

the game. The Crusaders' aggression at the tackle throughout the game was brutal, and so effective was their disruption at the breakdown that the Brumbies struggled to get over the gain line.

The Crusaders' players trust each other. There always seems to be someone there to support the ball carrier, which allows the side to string together phase upon phase. 'Communication is a huge part of the game,' said Mehrtens. When given free rein Mehrtens has a habit of creating the extraordinary. His all-round skills include decisive direction, soft, quick hands and an accurate kicking boot, but in the end it comes back to that sixth sense – an understanding between the players. 'And some of the responsibility comes down to the first five-eighth, who has to be talking really loudly to allow the half back to get in and throw the ball out without looking out for where you are, and that takes an extra split second off it as well,' commented Mehrtens. As this fly half has regularly demonstrated, fractions of time can turn games.

Deans said the Crusaders' mental strength and multiple levels of leadership had been crucial. Also no player would have the audacity to be selfish on the field because the team would not let that player get away with it. They are a close-knit group, and this feeling and spirit lies at the heart of Canterbury's fairy-tale dominance. The friendships and the enjoyment that the Crusaders share are obvious. 'We do a lot of hard work together, but there is a real equality in the team, no matter how much rugby experience you've had or what you've achieved you are on the same level as every other guy … the culture of taking the mickey out of each other really helps so that guys don't get too big for their boots,' Mehrtens said.

Of the other sides, the Waratahs made the semi-finals for the first time since the beginning of the Super 12 competition in 1997. This year they won their first five matches, including three away victories, two of which were in South Africa. The Highlanders finished fourth, maintaining their magnificent record at the 'House of Pain' in Dunedin, and completed the tournament boasting a rare win over the Brumbies in Canberra.

At the end of the season Mark McBain's reign as Queensland Reds coach came to an end after only two years when the Queensland Rugby Union decided against renewing his contract. McBain led the Reds to the Super 12 semi-finals in his first year in charge, while the team just missed the final four again this time, finishing fifth.

The Auckland Blues started the year strongly but lost their spark after speedy winger Rupeni Caucaunibuca suffered an injury that ended his season. The Stormers finished the strongest of the South African teams, in seventh spot. The Cape Town side were unlucky, losing two of their first four games by one point. The Chiefs winger Roger Randle was the competition's top try scorer, but that wasn't enough to boost his team, who finished eighth on the ladder. The Wellington Hurricanes may possess the awesome striking power of outside backs Jonah Lomu, Christian Cullen and Tana Umaga but were disappointing, scoring only two tries or less on seven out of eleven occasions. They were the lowest-placed New Zealand side.

The three cellar dwellers were South African teams. The Sharks lost skipper Mark Andrews and Butch James before the tournament began, and by the time the Durban side started to string together some wins at home it was too late. The Cats suffered with the departure of coach Laurie Mains and injuries to key back-rowers Andre Vos, Johan Erasmus and Andre Venter, and managed only one win from eleven matches. The lowly Bulls had 30 players and their coach leave from the team that played the previous season. They remain consistently the weakest team in the Super 12.

Given the Crusaders' authority in the Super 12 tournament, culminating in their awesome 31-13 triumph over former champions the ACT Brumbies, many argue that Canterbury are world rugby's champion provincial outfit and that the gap between the teams at the top of the table and those at the bottom is getting wider. While Canterbury are undoubtedly the best team there has been in the history of the Super 12 competition, they need to face the European Cup winners to decide if they are, in fact, as good as everyone in the southern hemisphere believes. A global play-off may be difficult to organise in an international rugby calendar that has become increasingly crowded, but if the idea captures the attention of the IRB it may become a regular fixture and settle the score.

**passenger request:** *Spoil me*

## Delta BusinessElite®:

*5 courses of tasty things to eat*
*a fine wine (or two)*
*all the films you've been meaning to see, TV and your kind of music*
*a serve yourself snack table*
*ice-cream sundaes so huge they're sinful*

▲**Delta**

fly **5-Star**

delta-air.com

# INTERNATIONAL SCENE

# Summer Tours 2002
## England in Argentina

### by ALASTAIR HIGNELL

'As England acclimatised in Buenos Aires, Grand Slam champions France were dumped on their derrières in front of a raucous, rapturous crowd at the Velez Sarsfield. The omens, to put it mildly, weren't good.'

It was hardly a 'tour to hell', but it could well have turned out to be a form of purgatory. Instead, an astonishing victory at the Velez Sarsfield stadium proved beyond doubt that a cupboard once deemed bare of reserves was now full to overflowing. England have a strength in depth that is the envy of their rivals and with just over a year until the World Cup have established a real competition for places. In the space of four years they have come a very long way indeed.

Back in 1998 England manager Clive Woodward took a grotesquely understrength squad to the southern hemisphere and saw his team at first humiliated, then, after four fairly comprehensive Test defeats, ridiculed. Now, with 30 senior players rested or injured after a season of punishing intensity, he was taking another bunch of rookies into the unknown, with very different results.

But right from the outset, the England manager was anxious to accentuate the positive. '1998 was a tour to hell in terms of results, not a nice experience at all, but the quality of player was totally different. This time we've got a far better group of players than we had four years ago, and even that tour threw up players like Jonny Wilkinson, Phil Vickery and Danny Grewcock, who are now household names.'

**LEFT** A delighted Clive Woodward celebrates with tour skipper Phil Vickery after England's 26-18 victory over the Pumas.

**RIGHT** Ben Kay touches down four minutes after the break for the first of England's two tries against Argentina.

A fortnight flit to Argentina may have held nowhere near the magnitude of terror of that month-long expedition of four years ago, but the Pumas had beaten Scotland and Wales in Europe the previous autumn before falling at home to the All Blacks by a single, late score. As England acclimatised in Buenos Aires, Grand Slam champions France were dumped on their derrières in front of a raucous, rapturous crowd at the Velez Sarsfield. The omens, to put it mildly, weren't good.

Even so, Woodward was undeterred. Before the tour he had called for two wins from two matches. Even though the A side were edged out by Argentina A on the Monday night, and even though the Pumas were cock-a-hoop after putting paid to France, the England manager insisted that they could be beaten. 'The team we've got is very young, and very inexperienced, but they're fresh and I think they will arguably put up a better job than those who are tired after the Lions tour. Provided they get the basics right at scrum, line out and at the turnover, I think they can win.'

Winning, as Woodward often stresses, is everything, but even he was not disingenuous enough to deny that he had another agenda on this tour. Increasingly, the playing calendar is defined by the World Cup, and the 2003 tournament in Australia is fast approaching. 'You've got to arrive at Rugby World Cup with a large group of experienced players. You can't get there with just 15 or 16 and hope to get through. That just doesn't happen. You do get injuries and you do need to play more than your starting XV in some of the other games. So, it's absolutely critical to develop a larger base. I have the nucleus of the World Cup squad in my mind, but there are gaps. That's why this game is so important. The players know that, but they also know the importance of winning. If they take care of that, then selection for the World Cup will take care of itself.'

While few outside the England camp could disagree with that sentiment, only one of the dozen or so journalists reporting on the trip could share the manager's faith in an England victory. Yet after surviving a bruising inquisition at the hands of the Puma set scrum, England turned in an inspired second half to turn around an interval deficit of 12-3. In the process they scored two superlative tries – through Ben Kay and debutant Phil Christophers – and then shut the Argentinians out with a measured and composed authority.

So, with victory taken care of, which players, if any, reinforced Woodward's World Cup thinking and which players forced him to revise it? While none of the players could be said to have taken a backward step either on the pitch or in the World Cup reckonings, those likely to have gained most would seem to be loose-head prop David Flatman, half backs Andy Gomarsall and Charlie Hodgson and wing Phil Christophers.

The Bristol flyer took his try with aplomb to prove that he has a big-match temperament to go with the versatility that has already seen him selected for his club at full back and centre. Flatman, whose break and beautifully weighted pass set Christophers free, looks set to push Graham Rowntree all the way in one of England's problem positions, while Gomarsall's continued renaissance will put huge pressure on England's most-capped scrum halves, Matt Dawson and Kyran Bracken. The 21-year-old Hodgson, in only his second full game at No. 10 for England, reassured Woodward that he has a ready-made understudy for the hitherto indispensable Jonny Wilkinson. Indeed, so well did Hodgson boss the game that Woodward could well be tempted to revisit the idea of switching his gold-plated goal-kicker to inside centre.

Of the others, Phil Vickery confirmed his status as a world-class forward, while Ben Kay took another giant leap towards greatness at lock. Lewis Moody gave more reasons for being considered ahead of Neil Back at open-side, while Alex Sanderson and Joe Worsley did enough to give Lawrence Dallaglio and Richard Hill a wake-up call they barely needed.

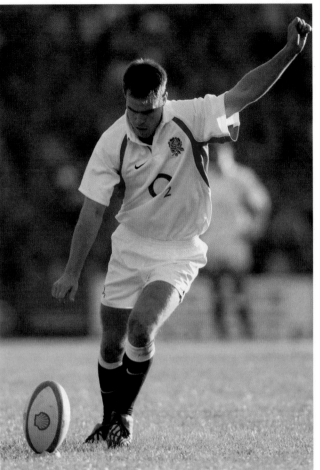

For Woodward, that, as well as the result, was just what the doctor ordered. 'A few of the guys at home will maybe have been watching the scenes and wishing maybe that they might have been here now. But you've just got to hand it to these fellows who did the business, and enjoy the achievement. The World Cup is a long, long way off yet.'

But approaching fast. And a significant number of those who do get to pull on the England jersey in Australia next autumn may well come to reflect that it all began in BA.

***ABOVE*** Stand-off Charlie Hodgson took charge of the game at the Velez Sarsfield, as well as converting England's two tries and kicking three penalties for a personal tally of 13 points.

***LEFT*** Loose-head prop David Flatman makes the break that set up England's second try against the Pumas, scored by Phil Christophers (right). Both players made strong cases in Argentina for consideration in Clive Woodward's World Cup plans.

# Scotland in North America

### by ALAN LORIMER

'After a 2002 championship characterised by drab play, Scotland desperately need to rebuild their side. The signs are that a number of players from their North America tour party are ready to step forward.'

Whatever positives may emerge from Scotland's six-match tour of North America in June, the public perception of this sortie to the New World will be strongly coloured by the Scots' 26-23 Test defeat by Canada at the Thunderbird Stadium in Vancouver. It was the only loss suffered by the Scots on tour, but this was the game that mattered and by which so much would be judged. In the event Scotland were found wanting against an unfancied Canadian side that contained five amateurs and ten players who had conceded over 100 points to Australia A prior to facing the Scots.

On paper this was the first official Test defeat of Scotland by Canada. But the same fate had befallen previous tour parties, most recently in 1991 when the Scots suffered a humiliation in New Brunswick in what was described as a non-cap match. Worse still for Scotland was the knowledge that only last year England's second stringers had put over 50 points past the Canadians in the Test at Vancouver. Scotland coach Ian McGeechan was, of course, able to plead the absence of many of his senior players, among them Scott Murray, Tom Smith and Budge Pountney. But five in the pack had played in the Six

Nations, while behind the scrum the line-up, which included Chris Paterson, Brendan Laney and Glenn Metcalfe, was arguably stronger than that fielded in the championship.

On the day – and a hot one it was in Vancouver – Scotland's forwards were outplayed by a Canadian pack sharper in winning ball on the ground. With little decent possession and less and less ball as the game ground on, Scotland's backs had few chances to show their skills and in the end were consigned to a defensive role. Galling for coach McGeechan was the way in which Scotland threw away a ten-point advantage after leading 23-13 at one stage. But even more frustrating was his charges' inability to make much headway against a Canadian side that was all guts and passion. Turnovers, lack of control at the breakdown and poor goal-kicking by Brendan Laney all contributed to a defeat in which the Scots outscored their opponents in tries by three to two.

Scotland's tries came from Chris Paterson, after an attempt by the Canadians to take a quick line out; scrum half Mike Blair from close range; and Simon Taylor, who barged over for his first score in international rugby. Canada trailed by just two points at the interval, with the scoreline at 15-13, having scored a try through Ulster-born No. 8 Phil Murphy, which was converted by stand-off Jared Barker, who also kicked two penalty goals. When the Scots extended their lead to 23-13 (helped by the sin-binning of Canadian skipper Al Charron), it seemed all over for the home side. Except that the Canadians had other ideas, translated into points with two penalty goals by Jared Barker and the stand-off's conversion of a try by prop John Thiel.

Amid the post-match glooom there were still a number of pluses to be taken from the game. Most notable was the performance at Test level of new scrum half Mike Blair, a newcomer to the professional ranks after playing for Boroughmuir last season. Blair, who was in Scotland's sevens squad as a teenager, has a sharp break, a swift service and a genuine tactical brain – all of which

adds up to a player ready to challenge for a regular place in the senior side. The other player to impress was Simon Taylor, the international No. 8 showing throughout the game a competitive attitude that contrasted so sharply with the tepid display of his colleagues. The Test also increased Scotland's official list of capped players. In addition to Blair, the new caps were wing Rory Kerr, centre Andy Craig, prop Craig Smith, flanker Donnie Macfadyen, utility back Ben Hinshelwood (whose father, Sandy, played for Scotland as a wing) and prop Allan Jacobsen.

What made the defeat all the more surprising was that a week earlier at Markham, near Toronto, the Scots had overwhelmed by 33-8 a Rugby Canada team which, with the exception of two players, was identically cast. Scotland's win in Markham was all

*BELOW* Flanker Allister Hogg runs away from USA A's Brian Surgener (left) and Matt Huckaby as Scotland's midweek side win 24-8 in Portland, Oregon.

*BELOW RIGHT* Lock Nathan Hines offloads out of the tackle against the Eagles in San Francisco. A try scorer in the win, Hines also became the first player to be sent off while playing for Scotland in an international.

about a controlled second-half performance in which the tourists scored four of their five tries. Winger Rory Kerr had touched down for Scotland's only first-half score, but from a potentially dangerous 8-8 half-time position the Scots drew away, adding tries by Mike Blair, Kerr, Duncan Hodge and Andy Craig.

Scotland's midweek side, meanwhile, had opened against Canada East with a 38-8 win in Kingston, Ontario, the only sour note being a tour-finishing injury to experienced flanker Martin Leslie. The midweekers remained unbeaten a week later after facing Canada West in Victoria, the second stringers emerging from a bruising battle with a 14-9 win. Prop Allan Jacobsen scored the tourists' only try. And it was the second stringers who were charged with putting Scotland's show back on the road after the shock Test defeat by Canada. In the event they duly restored the tourists' confidence with a 24-8 victory over USA A in Portland, Oregon. Four penalty goals by Ross and the stand-off's conversion of a Graeme Burns try gave Scotland a 19-3 lead, before a final attacking effort ended with Scotland Under 19 captain and flanker Allister Hogg scoring the tourists' second try.

So to the final match of the tour – the Test match against the USA at the Balboa Stadium in San Francisco. Scotland, determined to avoid a second consecutive Test defeat, were fired up for this game, albeit that it was the USA who struck first with a super try from winger Mose Timoteo. Thereafter Scotland, aided by some poor decision-making and weak tackling by a USA side playing its first Test match in six months, ran the show, piling up ten tries to finish winners 65-23. It was a purging performance, welding a silver lining to a dark, gloom-laden cloud that had descended a week earlier. Chris Paterson and Duncan Hodge each scored two tries, while the remainder came from Brendan Laney, Rory Kerr, Nathan Hines, Andrew Henderson, Andy Craig and Jason White.

The only blemish on Scotland's sparkling victory was the dismissal of Hines, the Australian-born lock becoming the first player in Scottish international rugby to be sent off. Hines' misdemeanour, a punch which flattened USA substitute Dan Anderson, was as palpable as it was historic, escaping neither the camera lens nor the eye of the touch judge. A further two players made debut appearances for Scotland – lock Andrew Hall, formerly of Moseley, and Marcus Di Rollo, the Edinburgh centre, making up to nine the number of new caps on the tour.

Overall, the positives from what was basically a developmental tour will surely outweigh the dispiriting defeat by Canada. One can recall a similar 'disaster' in Japan, on the 1989 summer tour. Then, a young winger called Tony Stanger emerged as a likely international player, fulfilling his potential nine months later with Murrayfield's most famous try in Scotland's 13-7 Grand Slam victory over England.

After a 2002 championship that was characterised by drab play, Scotland desperately need to rebuild their side. The signs are that a number of players from their North America tour party are ready to step forward. Apart from Blair, who was the number one success, Scotland coach Ian McGeechan must have been impressed with the form of winger Rory Kerr, rugby league convert Andy Craig at centre, prop Allan Jacobsen, teenage flanker Allister Hogg and lock Andrew Hall. McGeechan was also able to cast his eye over Ben Hinshelwood, Nikki Walker and Marcus Di Rollo in the backs, and Craig Smith, the powerful prop, among the forwards. These are players who may yet figure in Scotland's World Cup plans.

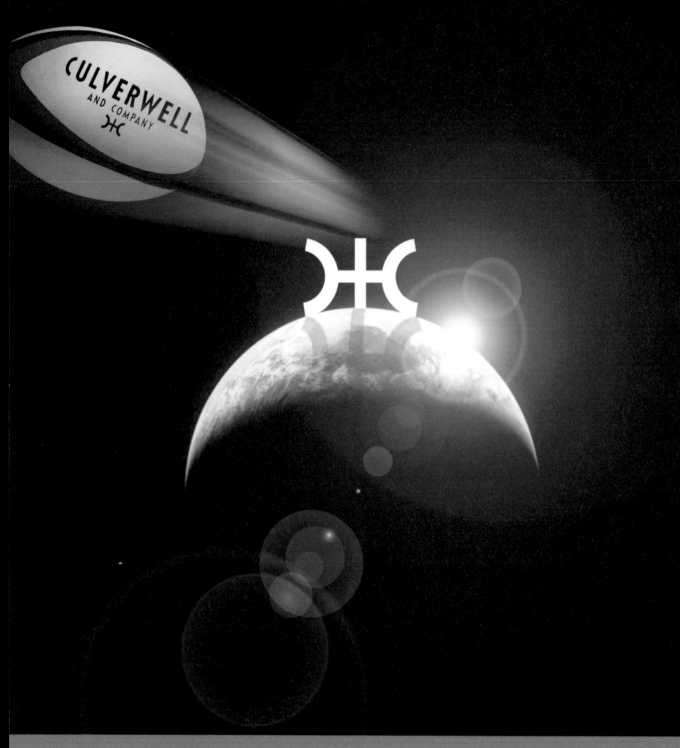

# You'll be converted

once you see how we go to the ends of earth and beyond to give you the best property advice in Scotland

## CULVERWELL
### AND COMPANY

# Wales in South Africa

## by GRAHAM CLUTTON

'The old faults are still there in terms of losing habits and a lack of confidence, but for the first time in a long time, there is a deep-seated feeling that the corner has been reached. Now, it's time to make that all important turn.'

For too long now, Welsh rugby, and its national team in particular, has been left to bemoan the one that got away. In South Africa this summer, the latest crop of international players suffered an all too familiar feeling of déjà vu. Admittedly, coming so close to beating South Africa on Springbok soil was significantly better than most of us foresaw when coach Steve Hansen and his able assistant Scott Johnson named a squad, which due to injury and unavailability, was missing several key elements. But rather than revel in the glory of relative success – two respectable defeats – the Class of 2002 have chosen to reflect on another series of missed opportunities, both in Bloemfontein, where a first-half lead was squandered, and in Cape Town, where the Springboks survived a torrid afternoon in the Cape rain before closing off the two-Test series in less than convincing fashion.

For Wales, the problems are of no small cause for concern. Of course there were positive signs and significant performances along the way – most notably from Michael Owen, Ryan Powell and Dwayne Peel – but right now, the losing habit runs deep through the collective vein of Welsh rugby's top players. Those near misses are no longer a coincidence. Missed opportunities are far too regular for anyone's liking, and unless fortunes change in the not too distant future, the habit will leave Welsh rugby skating on thin ice as it prepares for next year's Rugby World Cup.

However, before the executioner allows the blade to drop, Hansen, a former policeman and now a coach who has certainly endeared himself to the players during his short time in control, is planning to arrest the recent decline. And the coach is confident that in the wake of South Africa, the team management and the players who have come under so much pressure in recent times can plan ahead with real purpose. 'I said from the outset that I was more interested in the performance and attitude of the squad than anything else, but I was disappointed with the way we played ourselves into a position of strength and then gifted the Springboks successive victories,' said Hansen. 'That is the first lesson we have to learn. The performance in both games was adequate and at times we were dominant. That shows the depth of talent we have in the squad. But it's all about winning games from positions of strength and that was something we failed to do in both matches.'

With Scott Quinnell, Rob Howley, Andy Moore, Iestyn Harris, Darren Morris, Ian Gough, Chris Wyatt and Dafydd James missing for a variety of reasons, it was always likely to be a testing examination against a South Africa side that had a point to prove to themselves after such a dismal couple of seasons. But to a man – on and off the field – the side adapted well, played and trained with a real purpose and provided further confirmation that where there's a will there's a way. For 39 minutes in Bloemfontein, there was only one side in it. 'We defended well, showed great organisation and thoroughly deserved the try we scored through Craig Morgan. That was particularly pleasing,' said Hansen.

It was only after that that Hansen saw some of the old failings creeping in. Two Springbok tries in the closing moments of the half and a rather tame performance after the interval flattered South Africa as they won 34-19. In the end, it took a late consolation try from Rhys Williams to bring some respectability. Williams, like fellow Cardiff threequarter Craig Morgan and to an even greater extent Swansea full back Kevin Morgan, performed with real aplomb, suggesting that Messrs James and Gareth Thomas might have served their purpose.

**PREVIOUS PAGE** Wales flanker Michael Owen gathers at the line out in the first Test at Bloemfontein, which South Africa won 34-19. Owen one was of several players who impressed on tour and had a fine game in the second Test at Cape Town.

**RIGHT** Full back Brent Russell crosses at the end of the first half at Cape Town to score his first try for South Africa in his second international.

**BELOW** Wing Craig Morgan cracks the Springbok defence to open the scoring for Wales in the seventh minute at Bloemfontein.

A collective willingness to run rather than kick, step outside rather than back inside and an eye for the try line rather than the touch line will surely bring its reward as Wales gain more stability. Of course much will depend upon the forward contribution, but if parity can be gained in that department Wales possess a back three to match any in northern hemisphere rugby. 'We want to play an expansive game and we have runners who like to score tries,' said Hansen. 'If we can build on that, I think the side can turn these near misses into hits.'

When the side arrived back in Cape Town for the second Test at Newlands, there was a genuine feeling that they had missed the boat. Rudolf Straeuli, the Springbok coach, who, like Hansen, was feeling his way, had tested the water with half a dozen experiments and decided, after much deliberation, to revert to type for the second instalment. But just as the Springboks prepared with an air of confidence based on their second-half performance in Bloemfontein, so Wales felt that there was a definite Achilles' heel in the South African side. The challenge was exposing that. To their credit, as they had at Vodacom Park seven days previously, they found the weakness. 'That was pleasing,' said Hansen. 'I think most people had written us off after seeing us waste our first-half performance in Bloemfontein. But I had seen a resilience in the side and a definite edge in training that suggested we would cause problems.'

And that was very much the case. They were combative at the line out, where Gareth Llewellyn, Michael Owen and Steve Williams were head and shoulders above a disappointing Springbok line, and they were quick and eager on the floor, where Martyn Williams and Colin Charvis ruled supreme. Young scrum halves Dwayne Peel and Ryan Powell were also dominant figures, while Iestyn Thomas and Ben Evans were granite-like in their approach. Though defeat was again a bitter pill to swallow, it was a far cry from the mediocrity that had dominated the regular season, and at 8-8 Wales were odds-on to end their wait for a first win over the Springboks on South African soil.

But just as so many chances have gone begging before, so another came and went as the Boks won 19-8 with a late try from replacement scrum half Craig Davidson. The disappointment was clear, but when the dust settles on this short but almost very sweet summer excursion, Welsh rugby can look back with real optimism. The old faults are still there in terms of losing habits and a lack of confidence, but for the first time in a long time, there is a deep-seated feeling that the corner has been reached. Now, it's time to make that all important turn. Hansen will fashion a side based on youth as the countdown to next season's World Cup begins. Amen to that. And if it comes off, Wales will look back at this two-week tour as the first building block.

# REACH
# FOR THE
# BEST

It's rare to find a recruitment consultancy who tackle personnel requirements with such tenacity and unfailing dedication. An unrivalled approach that has enabled Pertemps to remain unchallenged at the top of the league as the UK's leading independent recruitment consultancy.

As market leaders, we have developed our reputation not just by "filling positions" but by adding value to our client portfolio, a philosophy which is reflected in the diverse range of leading blue-chip companies that currently utilise our services.

Operating in three service divisions: commercial and professional, industrial and driving and technical and executive, our fully integrated service ensures that we are able to deliver quality personnel with the right skills, in the right place at the right time.

So, if you are seeking to win the competition for business, make sure that you retain the competition for talent by choosing Pertemps, Britain's most successful independent recruitment consultancy.

## PERTEMPS
*recruitment partnership*

**HEAD OFFICE:**
**Meriden Hall, Main Road, Meriden,**
**Warwickshire CV7 7PT.**
**Tel: 01676 525000  Fax: 01676 525009**
Email: info@pertemps.co.uk
Web Site: www.pertemps.co.uk

# Ireland in New Zealand

## by SEAN DIFFLEY

'In the circumstances, then, the Irish, who appeared to have been thrown to the wolves, didn't do badly. In fact they could have made history and won the first Test in Dunedin.'

The decision that Ireland tour New Zealand in the summer of 2002 and play two Tests may well have been made in the enthusiastic days when Captain Cook sailed in that area. But after a hard, long and tough home season, it was a bit like prolonging the agony for the Irish rugby squad. And though he was too polite to say it, clearly coach Eddie O'Sullivan would have much preferred to summer on the beaches around Galway Bay than on the sand of Timaru, where tour affairs began with a comprehensive win over a New Zealand Divisional XV by 54-3.

And a certain degree of, er, importance, too, was attached to the number of injured players who were unable to accept their invitations to travel. The list comprised Denis Hickie, Rob Henderson, Jeremy Davidson, Kevin Maggs, Shane Horgan and Anthony Horgan. Called up were Mel Deane of Sale, Tyrone Howe and the Munster wing John Kelly, who was to gain his first cap and end up playing in both Tests in the centre.

In the circumstances, then, the Irish, who appeared to have been thrown to the wolves, didn't do badly. In fact they could have made history and won the first Test in Dunedin. As it was they lost 15-6, and if they did not do quite enough to deserve a win, the nine points winning margin rather flattered the All Blacks. And at the end the 40,000 crowd at Carisbrook roundly booed their team – an all-Canterbury side, which may have inspired the reaction.

It was 10-3 to the All Blacks at half-time, Ireland's score coming from an early dropped goal by Brian O'Driscoll, while Mehrtens kicked a penalty for the All Blacks and converted wing Doug Howlett's try after 34 minutes. Ireland had more than their fair share of possession in the closing minutes and were only 6-10 behind, but it was the All Blacks who wrapped it up. Centre Aaron Mauger chipped ahead and full back Leon MacDonald got over the

Irish line after substitute wing Jonah Lomu (he came on after 67 minutes) had evaded three Irish tackles.

Ronan O'Gara, though he ran the back line with considerable thought and courage, had a bad day with his place-kicking. Both he and his New Zealand opposite number, Andrew Mehrtens, found the 'new' ball presented by Adidas, the All Blacks' kit sponsors, difficult to kick. A 'yellow submarine' they dubbed it. It is a matter that should concentrate the minds of the IRB, who must, surely, rule that a universally accepted ball be used for all internationals.

The Irish certainly gained credit for running the All Blacks so close considering the pre-tour problems. But it was a different story the following week in Auckland, when the All Blacks hit back with a vengeance and demolished the Irish 40-8 – and it was Keith Wood's 50th cap, too.

Five tries to one tells its own story, with four of New Zealand's scores coming in the second half. This time Lomu was an original selection, infiltrating the Canterbury pick. The Irish forwards did well enough in the first half, but the backs displayed an astonishing lack of cohesion. Ireland's only score in that period was yet another dropped goal from O'Driscoll. Late in the second half, lock Gary

---

***ABOVE LEFT***  Ireland full back Girvan Dempsey seizes the 'yellow submarine' as All Black centre Aaron Mauger looks on during the first Test at Carisbrook, Dunedin.

***ABOVE RIGHT***  Geordan Murphy is unable to stop Caleb Ralph scoring in the corner in New Zealand's five-try win in the second Test at Auckland.

***RIGHT***  A buried Byron Kelleher looks up as he scores a minute after replacing Justin Marshall at Auckland.

***PREVIOUS PAGE***  Ireland No. 8 Anthony Foley charges upfield during the first Test at Carisbrook, Dunedin.

Longwell stretched over for a try which O'Gara failed to convert, as he had with three feasible penalties earlier. The infamous 'yellow submarine' again! The five New Zealand tries came from MacDonald, who scored two, wing Caleb Ralph, replacement scrum half Byron Kelleher from Otago, who crossed after just one minute on the pitch, and Marty Holah, another replacement. Mehrtens penalties and conversions did the rest.

So, in two Test matches the Irish managed two dropped goals, one penalty and one try for a total of 14 points – not the most glorious of visits. There is no doubt that it was a tour too far, and that this was probably so was realised long before the squad departed Down Under. It underlined, once again, the current tendency in the game to overplay the players. The break after a long season was much too short, and sooner or later the IRB will have to do something drastic about the situation.

Any positives, then, for Ireland coach Eddie O'Sullivan to take into next season and the Six Nations Championship? Peter Clohessy has retired and was not on the tour, but the performance of Richie Corrigan, Leinster's captain last season, was excellent in all the circumstances and he may well fill the gap adequately at loose-head prop.

# Black Fern Spring
## the 2002 Women's World Cup

by PAUL MORGAN

'The IRB didn't do enough to promote the game in the Spanish city, and it is clear that for the 2006 event they either need to pump greater resources into the Women's World Cup or offer it to a developed rugby nation who can do that for themselves.'

The battle for the fourth Women's World Cup was always going to come down to a head-to-head between New Zealand and England, and so it proved. In an event staged against the sensational backdrop of Barcelona, the New Zealand Black Ferns cast a shadow over the tournament from the moment they started their title defence with a 117-0 hammering of Germany.

England closed the gap on the Kiwis, who didn't concede a try in the whole tournament, but it is still the Black Ferns who lead the way and set the standards in the women's game. No other side mounted a serious challenge to the big two, and they produced a final of supreme quality that took the women's game to a new level.

Unfortunately for England they left their best form behind in the semi-finals, in which they hammered Canada 53-10 with a performance full of power and pace. A similar display in the final could have wrested the trophy from the Kiwis. Nevertheless England were never overwhelmed by the Kiwis and stayed within a score of the world champions until very late in the game, which took place in front of a noisy 8000-strong crowd in the Olympic Stadium.

But the Black Ferns played like their male All Black counterparts to win the final 19-9. Their attack was incisive and their defence held firm as it had done throughout the tournament. 'The girls didn't want to let the jersey down,' explained New Zealand coach Daryl Suasua. 'It is the power of the black jersey. It comes from the tradition of what the men had set. We took a long look at the All Blacks' history and what it meant but the Black Ferns now have their own history.'

Player of the match was clearly Black Ferns scrum half Monique Hirovanaa, who scored one try and made another with a scintillating break from half way. 'I knew I really had to pull out a big one against England,' she said . 'We did a lot of homework on England and they probably played into our hands a fair bit. The gap I ran through to make the second try you could have driven a bus through it. They've got a big forward pack and their scrum went pretty well too, but we knew they would try to rumble through us up front and we were waiting for them. I think we really pounced on them defensively and hit back hard, and that was what won it for us in the end.'

England captain Paula George couldn't have asked more of her side, who in 2001 had managed to inflict New Zealand's first defeat in a decade. She said: 'I am so proud of this team. I wouldn't swap any of the 26-player squad. The final was a fantastic advert for the women's game. Women's rugby has come on much in the last four years and I'm convinced it will continue to grow.'

France – the 2002 Grand Slam champions – were unlucky to be seeded fourth, and therefore collided with the Kiwis in the semi-finals, losing 30-0 in Cornella. Scotland achieved their objective in finishing sixth but know they are a long way behind the improving Australians, who beat them in the plate final in Girona. The Scots once again proved they have a pack to live with the best, but the Australian backs proved too powerful. Kazakhstan were competing for the third time. Having finished ninth in 1998, they dropped back to eleventh in 2002 but enjoy the unique distinction of being the only country where women's rugby has overtaken the men's game in terms of development.

**ABOVE** The New Zealand Black Ferns with the Women's World Cup and their winner's medals after their 19-9 defeat of England in the final.

**PREVIOUS PAGE** Player of the final Black Ferns scrum half Monique Hirovanaa brings down England's Selena Rudge.

As at all World Cups a number of the big names treated it as their swansong. Two of the pioneers of the women's game, Liza Burgess of Wales and Gill Burns of England, confirmed their international retirement plans within hours of the tournament finishing. Burgess helped Wales to their highest finish at the World Cup, tenth, although she finished with a defeat as her side lost the bowl final 17-14 to Samoa. Burgess' incredible international career has spanned 15 years and brought the Clifton lock 71 caps. She said: 'It's one better than 1998 but we were extremely disappointed not to go out with the bowl trophy. We did our homework on the Samoans, and after wins over Germany [75-0] and Italy [35-3] we were confident of making it three wins in a row, as we thought we had done enough. But I look back on my international career with great affection and I'm now focusing on a new start at Clifton.

'The commitment involved and the standards of play have altered a lot. When I first started playing we didn't have that many international fixtures, whereas now the season is more or less ten months of the year. I've been training quite hard since I was at university, though, and we're given so much more information and support now that it's not hard to motivate myself. The future of Welsh rugby is really exciting and I am involved with coaching the Under 16s squad, which I greatly enjoy. There are some really talented players coming through at youth level and I am so excited about seeing them play senior rugby.' Burgess' sadness, though, was joy for the Samoans, who at their first Women's World Cup excelled to lift the bowl trophy.

Burns's England made it to the final, although she herself wasn't used in the game against New Zealand until the dying minutes. In the semi-final against Canada, however, Burns produced one of the performances of her career, combining with Emma Mitchell to form a platform for England that took them to their 53-10 victory.

Although the players enjoyed things on the field, many left disappointed with the profile the tournament achieved and the organisation of it. The IRB didn't do enough to promote the game in the Spanish city, and it is clear that for the 2006 event they either need to pump greater resources into the Women's World Cup or offer it to a developed rugby nation who can do that for themselves.

Most of the games were watched by crowds that were so small it devalued the huge effort put in by the players and management of all 16 sides. I can understand the need to bring a tournament of this size to a developing rugby nation like Spain, but it must arrive with enough money to promote and market it. The Women's World Cup can no longer be considered alongside the Under 21 or Under 19 competitions for the men – it is much bigger than these. And the same goes for referees. They can no longer come to the Women's World Cup for experience. The tournament needs officials from among the top ten in the world.

Australian Rugby Union chief executive John O'Neill has declared that to promote the Rugby World Cup they need to 'spend a dollar to make a dollar'. And the same must be true for the 2006 Women's World Cup. In Barcelona they didn't even seem to be using simple promotional techniques such as bussing in schoolchildren to watch the games. The matches were scheduled, and the crowds – as in rugby union 20 years ago – were left to their own devices about whether they turned up. The men's game has quickly learnt the power of the marketeer, and the women's game must do the same, although it has no chance without money from the IRB.

The tournament was about far more than the action on the field. On one of the free days more than 50 delegates from 20 countries took part in the IRB Women's Conference. The items discussed included recruitment, sevens as a vehicle for promotion and development, the development of the women's game from U16 to adult, coach and referee development and challenges facing the top level of the women's game. Geoff Evans, the IRB development manager, said: 'There was a consensus that the IRB had already played a pivotal part in this growth but that it needed to continue to reassess the way in which issues such as coaching and refereeing were further developed.'

Evans is right about that pivotal role, but the next stage is crucial, and the IRB need to make sure they give the women the tournament they deserve in 2006.

# The Story So Far
# Rugby World Cup 2003

## by CHRIS THAU

'Without doubt the Repechage, with two final berths at stake in Pool B and Pool D, will emerge as one of the most exciting contests in the qualifiers, as the standard of the participating teams is fairly close.'

As the qualifying process for RWC 2003 edges towards its final stages the shape of the tournament draw is emerging. The first of the 12 qualifiers to book their tickets for Australia were Fiji and Samoa, the winners and runners-up of the Oceania zone. Fiji and Samoa each won three and lost one, but the Fijians won the pool on account of a superior points margin. As a result Fiji took the Oceania 1 berth in Pool B alongside France and Scotland, while the Samoans qualified as Oceania 2 in the so-called 'Pool of Death' dominated by South Africa and England.

Tonga, who finished third in Oceania, have to relaunch their bid for a place in the RWC 2003 finals in Round 3 of the qualifying zone. Here they will meet the winners of Round 1, Papua New Guinea and Cook Islands – who took a bye in Round 2 – for a place in the Repechage. Local pundits who saw the young Tongan team in action against both Samoa and Fiji argue that 'Ikale Tahi' have the potential to go all the way as one of the Repechage finalists, though the Cook Islands and Papua New Guinea may have a different opinion.

In Asia, the last of the IRB zones to start the qualifying process, the new-look Japan have all but secured themselves the lucrative Asian slot in Pool B of the Australian line-up. At the time of writing they still had a match to play against Korea in Seoul but had built such a commanding lead in their previous three matches that their presence as Asia 1 alongside the Scots, French and Fijians was all but a forgone conclusion. The ruthless manner of Japan's 90-24 demolition of Korea – once their challenger for Asian supremacy – as well as a host of earlier results, including the humiliation of Russia in Tokyo, suggest that under new coach Shogo Mukai, Japan have finally managed to cross the threshold into the realm of rugby prominence.

Their new playing style is a blend of Japan's traditional features – speed of action and thought, elusiveness and courage – with power play and, significantly, an ability to vary both pace and tactics. And just to prove the point, their subsequent 23-try, 155-3 Tokyo annihilation of Chinese Taipei – historically one of their awkward opponents in Asia – has confirmed Japan's status as the continent's superpower, while setting numerous new records in the process. To add insult to injury, they beat Chinese Taipei 120-3 in the return, for the highest aggregate home-and-away score in RWC history.

The Russians, who visited Japan for a friendly in May as a preparation for the final round of the European qualifiers, have been trying to comprehend the causes of their 50-point drubbing. 'We came to Japan confident that we had improved after the European Nations Cup competition this year, but Japan's work rate and inventiveness overwhelmed us. We made too many mistakes in defence, which cost us dearly. But this is not the end of the world. It is very useful to have such matches before our crucial qualifying games in RWC 2003,' Russian captain Roman Romak said.

The Russians compete for one of the four RWC 2003 final berths at stake in Europe. Ireland and Italy are naturally favourites to go through (as Europe 1 and 2), with Romania, Georgia, Russia and Spain, in that order, battling for the remaining two positions. Georgia and Russia join Ireland in Pool One of Round 4, while Italy entertain Romania and Spain in the other pool. RWC planners seeding the teams for Round 3 Europe had used the outcome of the 2002 European Nations Cup (ENC). ENC winners Romania and runners-up Georgia got a bye and qualified directly for Round 4 alongside

**RIGHT** Nicolas Grille of Uruguay on the rampage against rivals Chile.

**BELOW RIGHT** Portugal on the attack during the match in Madrid that saw Spain progress to Round 4 Europe.

Italy and Ireland, while Russia, Netherlands, Portugal and Spain joined Poland and the Czech Republic in Round 3.

The Russians won their Round 3 pool, in which they were pitted against the Czechs and the Netherlands, with comparative ease, which granted them the right to host the Irish and travel to Tbilisi for the Round 4 Pool One decider, with a place in the Sydney starting line-up at stake. Russia's South African coach James Stoffberg has unearthed and subsequently signed several provincial-standard South African players of Russian descent, and as a result Russia's comprehension and their ability to play expansive rugby has considerably increased. While within the IRB regulations, the Russian foray into foreign markets has not been universally applauded in Europe and, as critics point out, it is unlikely to help the development of the Russian game in the long term. The Georgians are aware of the magnitude of the task ahead, and their president, Bidzina Gegidze, put it in a nutshell when he observed: 'All we must do now is to concentrate on beating our arch-rivals Russia in the autumn for a place in Sydney'.

Spain, on the other hand, reached Round 4 thanks to a genuine act of escapism. The Spanish lost to Poland 27-15, and with the Portuguese just managing to beat the rampant Poles in Lisbon, they won their passage to Round 4 against their Iberian neighbours in Madrid. The Romanians, under their new French coach Bernard Charreyre and fired up by their success in the European Nations Cup, are aware that a win against Italy, away from home, may be beyond their present capabilities, but Spain at home should definitely be within their grasp.

The African zone ends in the autumn with the two play-offs between Southern Africa champions Namibia and Tunisia, winners of the North African pool. In the Southern Africa sub-zone Namibia and Zimbabwe between them burst the Madagascar bubble, though the achievements of Madagascan rugby in reaching

the fourth round should not be underestimated. Namibia, fielding for the first time a team close to its potential, bulldozed their way through to a century of points (112-0) against Madagascar, followed by a 42-30 defeat of a talented Zimbabwe team in Bulawayo for a place in the all-Africa final.

Tunisia, on the other hand, the eternal underachievers of North African rugby, have avenged years of failed chances, narrow defeats and humiliating exits from various competitions at the hands of their arch-rivals Morocco and Côte d'Ivoire with a historic one-point win over Morocco at the Chedly Zouiten stadium in Tunis. 'This is the stuff that dreams are made of,' said match hero Kais Aissa at the end of a pulsating encounter which left virtually all 5000 spectators – a new record for an international rugby match in Tunis – emotionally drained. On the strength of their earlier performances Namibia are hot favourites to capture the Africa 1 berth in Pool A, but Tunisia's track record as giant-killers should not be dismissed out of hand.

By beating the USA both home and away, the Canadians have taken a seemingly unassailable two-match lead in the qualifying race against the Eagles, Chile and Uruguay. After earlier upheavals Canada, fielding a settled side under coach David Clark, are likely to end up in Pool D as America 1, with the Eagles battling Uruguay's Los Teros and Chile's Los Cóndores for the remaining American slot in Pool C. Chile's campaign began in São Paulo, where they beat Brazil 46-6, and finished with a 57-5 win against Paraguay in Santiago. Predictably, the Brazilian RWC dream – which with the play-offs against Trinidad and Tobago went further then

> ## THE STORY SO FAR
>
> *The emerging line-up for the RWC 2003 finals in Australia at the time of writing was as follows:*
>
> ### Pool A
> Australia
> Argentina
> Ireland
> Namibia/Tunisia
> Russia/Georgia
>
> ### Pool B
> France
> Scotland
> Fiji
> Japan
> Tonga/Africa 2/America 3/Europe
>
> ### Pool C
> South Africa
> England
> Samoa
> Romania
> USA
>
> ### Pool D
> New Zealand
> Wales
> Italy
> Canada
> Russia/Georgia/Africa 2/America 3

anything Mario Dominguez and his men had expected – ended at the hands of the ruthless Cóndores, led by their evergreen captain, Alfonso Escobar, who was enticed out of retirement by new coach Jorge Navesi. However, the comfortable margins have not lulled Los Cóndores into a false sense of security. 'Canada and USA are a different kind of challenge because we have never played against them and we don't have that love-hate relationship we have with Uruguay. The Chilean side is now more experienced with many of the players who felt frustrated by the narrow Uruguay defeat four years ago prepared to go the extra mile, this time, to hopefully turn despair into joy.' Escobar said.

A win against Uruguay will send the Chileans into the Repechage, alongside the Koreans, the winner of the Tonga/Cook Islands/Papua New Guinea triangular, the winner of the European play-off between the third-placed teams in the two pools (Georgia/Russia v Romania/Spain), and the losers of the African Tunisia v Namibia play-off. However, the odds are heavily stacked against them making further progress, as Los Teros have been assiduously preparing for the Pan-American qualifying series.

While Korea's 119-7 defeat of Chinese Taipei in Round 4 of the Asian zone is unlikely to affect the outcome of the pool, it might give Korean confidence a timely boost before the crucial encounter against the winner of Round 3 Oceania in the Repechage. Without doubt the Repechage, with two final berths at stake in Pool B and Pool D, will emerge as one of the most exciting contests in the qualifiers, as the standard of the participating teams is fairly close.

# All Black Hat-trick
## the 2001-02 IRB World Sevens

by **ALAN LORIMER**

'If the adage of being as good as your last success holds true, then New Zealand can take much out of their win at Cardiff. With the title already in the bag at Kuala Lumpur and with distinct signs of campaign fatigue evident in the squad, Tietjens' boys still managed to hold off an England side that had been growing in confidence.'

Once they had built up that familiar head of steam there was never any doubt that New Zealand would claim the IRB World Sevens Series title for the third successive year. Few would have expected a different outcome from the country that pioneered the concept of a dedicated sevens squad, but at least the landscape is now changing, with new challengers emerging in the abbreviated game. The moment of triumph for New Zealand occurred in Kuala Lumpur, where the All Blacks, at the end of another tournament-winning performance, moved into unassailable territory to confirm themselves as champions yet again.

Victory in Malaysia had put New Zealand on a points total of 158 and out of reach of the chasing Springboks. With two tournaments – in London and Cardiff – still remaining it might have been the chance for the All Blacks to ease off, but predictably the response from coach Gordon Tietjens was quite the opposite. 'We'll try to win them both,' said Tietjens, in something of a prescient statement. The All Blacks duly carried out Tietjens' wishes, surging to victory first at Twickenham and then at the Millennium Stadium to make it seven wins in the eleven-tournament series. The final tally for New Zealand showed the All Blacks victorious at Durban, Santiago, Beijing, Singapore, Kuala Lumpur, London and Cardiff. At the conclusion of the Cardiff tournament Tietjens summed up his side's achievement. He said: 'It's pleasing to win with so many rookies in the squad. They've done very well.'

Among the new players to impress were Anthony Tuitavake, whose blistering pace was crucial in the Twickenham final against South Africa, and teenager Joe Rokocoko, who has made the transition from youth player to senior sevens specialist with ease. However, Fijian-born Rokocoko, who joined the sevens squad after playing for New Zealand Schools last season, was to miss the Commonwealth Games sevens tournament following his injury in the IRB Under 21 Championship in Johannesburg.

**PREVIOUS PAGE** North Harbour flyer Anthony Tuitavake showed himself to be one of the emerging stars of New Zealand sevens during the 2001-02 competition.

**OPPOSITE PAGE** Quins speedster Ben Gollings in action for England at HQ, with Henry Paul in support. Gollings was a try scorer in England's win over Fiji in the Hong Kong final.

**BELOW** South Africa captain Paul Treu leaves the French defence in his wake during the Twickenham tournament, in which the Boks finished as runners-up to New Zealand.

Despite New Zealand's ultimately large margin of victory, there were several disappointments for the All Blacks. The major glitches were at Brisbane, Wellington and Hong Kong, where rivals – sounding Commonwealth Games warnings – ruined the party. At Ballymore it was the host country, Australia, who destroyed New Zealand with a 28-0 win in the final, while a week later in Wellington, South Africa downed the All Blacks with a 26-10 win in the final.

For the Springboks, the win in Wellington was not entirely unexpected, their overall second-place finish in the IRB World Series confirming the huge improvement made by the Boks. With scorching pace thoughout their side and big-time performers like Egon Seconds, Anton Pitout, Paul Treu, and Marius Schoeman in the squad to complement the finishing of Brent Russell, the Springboks, coached by the legendary Chester Williams, repaid the South African Rugby Union's investment in creating a full-time sevens squad.

Hong Kong revealed another fast-improving country as England overcame the difficult conditions to beat once-invincible Fiji by 33-20 in the final, the Fijians having disposed of New Zealand in the semi-finals with a 10-7 win. If the adage of being as good as your last success holds true, then New Zealand can take much out of their win at Cardiff. With the title already in the bag at Kuala Lumpur and with distinct signs of campaign fatigue evident in the squad, Tietjens' boys still managed to hold off an England side that had been growing in confidence.

Under coach Joe Lydon, the former Great Britain rugby league star, England, after a slow start, simply got better and better. It is a credit to Lydon that he produced such fine results while operating with a squad that changed from tournament to tournament. But at least the agreement between the RFU and the Premiership clubs ensured that quality players were available for IRB tournaments even if consistency was absent. Other than the Hong Kong performance, Cardiff was England's other top showing. Lydon moulded another new side into a team that gave the All Blacks a genuine run for their money. In a throwback to England's 1993 World Cup win at Murrayfield, Lydon showed that using genuine forwards was still a shrewd modus operandi even if just about every other country was using backs in the forward trio.

England's use of Phil Greening's specialist hooking skills secured crucial tight-head strikes, while Pat Sanderson, revelling in the sevens game after an injury-interrupted season, proved that a ball-winning forward is just as vital in the abbreviated game as in fifteens. Behind the scrum, Nick Duncombe emerged as an accomplished link player and a skilful sweeper, Ben Gollings provided attacking flair, Henry Paul supplied a commanding presence, and Richard Haughton and Paul Sampson possessed sufficient pace to match the quickest in the game.

England's rise coincided with the relative demise of Fiji. The sevens magicians, it seems, have met their match as other countries have applied professionalism to counter amateur brilliance. A fourth-place finish would have been unthinkable in the past. Fiji are no longer the power they once were. Among the other countries to impress were Samoa, always capable of causing an upset; the unpredictable French, for whom sevens could be the ultimate platform for their sheer flair; and Argentina, whose finest tournament was in Singapore, where they lost narrowly to New Zealand in the final.

Wales, despite a poor performance in front of their own crowd in Cardiff, finished eighth overall and crucially developed a number of young players, among them winger Craig Richards. Under coach Colin Hillman, Wales produced their best form in Hong Kong, where they reached the semi-finals. Scotland, inventors of the short game, finally convinced themselves that they should take sevens more seriously, and while not showing the commitment of Wales, still managed to compete in six of the IRB tournaments, their best performances being in Hong Kong, Singapore and Cardiff.

The beauty of sevens is that it allows smaller and emerging rugby nations to compete. You only have to look at the results to appreciate that for the likes of Paraguay, Cook Islands, Kenya, and Trinidad sevens is a chance to be seen on the world stage. Sevens is also taken seriously in Russia, Georgia, Spain and Portugal, and if you think soccer totally dominates in South Korea then think again. Rugby sevens is proving to be a successful world sport confirming what we have thought all the time. Small, indeed, is beautiful.

Some things get better given longer.

Brewed longer
for a distinctive,
full flavour.

ABBOT ALE

# A Talent Conveyor Belt
## the International Youth Tournaments
by CHRIS THAU

'It is now accepted that the success rate of the Under 19 World Championship is measured, in most participating nations, by the number of talented youngsters it provides to the elite programme, and not by medals and cups.'

Unlike the senior Rugby World Cup, which allows the victorious team to bask in the glory of being world champions for four long years, the Under 19 and Under 21 world championships are annual developmental competitions, where work for the next event begins on the day the matches of the present one come to an end. Under 18 competitions are already being played in all IRB regions to identify the four qualifiers for the Under 19 World Championship B Division in 2003; beneath, the Under 17 age group provides the elite developmental pyramid with a wider base. The introduction of the IRB Under 21 World Cup (heir to the SANZAR/UAR Under 21 Tournament) and its equivalent Under 20 feeder system has provided the world of rugby with an uninterrupted conveyor belt for talent.

It is now accepted that the success rate of the Under 19 World Championship is measured, in most participating nations, by the number of talented youngsters it provides to the elite programme, and not by medals and cups. But it is not the competition in itself that enables the 90-odd IRB Unions to find talented youngsters for the game. In the world's leading rugby nations, players can reach the top via different channels and development programmes; in the emerging nations, the programme centred on the Under 19 World Championship is the key to the success, and sometimes survival, of senior rugby. It is the talent identification programmes and selection systems set in place for the tournament that keep the system working, improving the number of quality players reaching the higher echelons of the game. The role of the Under 21 age group is to further fine-tune the system, with the number of players reaching the senior national team as the measure of the success rate. The recently introduced Under 21 World Cup will further the scope for development in the rest of the world and will lead to an upsurge in standards and quality.

However, the 34th World Junior Championship (IRB/FIRA U19 World Championship), held in the northern Italian region of Treviso, near Venice, will not be remembered for the remarkable quality displayed by the 32-strong field, although many of the participating nations – notably Russia, Georgia, England, Japan, Italy, Scotland, Canada, Spain, newcomers Namibia, the USA, Paraguay, Chile and Uruguay – made vast strides forward in terms of skill, organisation and comprehension. What will stay in the collective memory of the 10,000 spectators gathered in Treviso's main rugby stadium for the tournament final will be the distressing degree of the demolition of France by arguably the most outrageously talented New Zealand youth team in years.

It was not the fact that New Zealand had acquired the coveted Under 19 World Championship shield for the third time in four appearances since 1999 that surprised the pundits. After all, New Zealand were the reigning champions, having won the previous year in Santiago. What raised eyebrows and made spectators hold their breath in sheer awe was the outstanding ability of the young Blacks to clinically dismantle seemingly locked defences, glide through tackles and defensive platforms with frightening ease and score at will. Credit to their coaches Aussie McLean and Leicester Rutledge, the New Zealanders produced a sizzling mix of pace, power, skill and footballing nous that set them apart. Sadly, but amazingly, there was never any doubt at the start of their matches, with perhaps one exception, about who was going to win – only about the margin of victory.

That one exception was the young Springbok side. Had the team under the guidance of Oersond Gorgonzola, Chris van Loggerenberg and Andre Eloff concentrated on the efficient and perhaps dull ten-man rugby they could perform to perfection, South Africa would have been in with a chance. The only time New Zealand looked rattled was when South African captain Luke Watson and his team-mates laboured their way upfield with an interminable series of mauls and rushes close to the pack. But instead of persevering in battering their opponents into submission, when they were in the New Zealand 22 South Africa spun the ball wide, with devastating consequences for their designs. The ball ended invariably in New Zealand hands, and reasonably often behind South Africa's line. This was, by and large, the story of every single New Zealand match in the tournament.

All this is now history, and the rugby world has commenced working for the 35th tournament scheduled for France in March 2003. 'Having missed the 2001 Under 19 World Championship, the immediate impact the [2002] tournament has had on me was to note the vast improvement in the standard of play in the lower reaches of Division 1 and the upper echelons of Division 2. This was enhanced by a great improvement in the fitness of teams, in spite of a very taxing playing schedule over two weeks. The level of fitness resulted in greater accuracy in the performance of the skills of the game, in particular, passing, tackling and ball retention. The contest for possession, especially the line out, was particularly pleasing. It takes a lot of work for teams to ensure scrum stability and to develop the skills to compete for the ball in the line out and not just concede possession and contest territory,' was the verdict of former IRB development manager Lee Smith.

The first SANZAR/UAR Southern Hemisphere Under 21 Tournament, the forefather of the Under 21 World Cup, was the brainchild of Carlos Tozzi, long-time UAR president and an IRB council member. At the beginning of 1995 the four Unions concerned – South Africa, New Zealand, Australia and Argentina – agreed to stage the Under 21 tournament in Buenos Aires. The tournament was an instant hit, and the four never looked back.

A talent-loaded New Zealand team, with the likes of Taine Randell, Anton Oliver, Christian Cullen, Carl Hoeft, Kees Meeuws, Scott Robertson and Carlos Spencer in their ranks, coached by Ross Cooper and Lin Colling and led by Randell with Oliver as his able lieutenant, were outstanding throughout. 'That team was the basis of the All Black team of the next few years and the tournament was a great learning curve for all involved,' coach Lin Colling observed.

Not only the All Blacks benefited. Tom Bowman, Toutai Kefu, Nathan Grey, Justin Harrison and Bill Young were the future Wallabies among the Under 21s coached by Ian Kennedy and Geoff Richards, while Robbie Kempson, Selborne Boome, Andre Snyman and Breyton Paulse eventually became Springboks. Last but not least, Argentina, captained by Santiago Phelan, had Gonzalo Quesada, Ignacio Fernandez Lobbe and Gonzalo Longo among the stars of the future. Overall, 34 players from that inaugural tournament – a remarkable 32 per cent of the total number – went on to win international honours: 33 represented participating countries, while one was capped by Italy.

The next tournament, held in New Zealand, created the legend of the Under 21s and convinced the 'shareholders' to carry on with it. The home side – with Anton Oliver as captain, Tony Brown,

Andrew Blowers, Norm Maxwell and Greg Feek – were odds-on to retain the trophy. But the Australians, featuring a host of future Wallabies – Nathan Grey, Chris Latham, Elton Flatley, Sam Cordingley and Tom Bowman – begged to differ, and with 'veteran' skipper Grey scoring in the dying seconds of a passionate encounter they prevailed 17-14 to silence the partisan New Zealand crowd and take the trophy to Sydney.

A year later, the same four nations gathered in Sydney, and the hosts successfully defended the silver bowl. The unusual feature of that Under 21 Australian team was that it produced not only future Wallabies but also players who represented Ireland (Keith Gleeson), Wales (Jason Jones-Hughes) and Samoa (Fosi Pa'alamo). Twelve players from the Argentina Under 21 side in that tournament went on to represent their country. Overall 41 players (the Argentinians plus ten Australians, eleven New Zealanders and eight South Africans) from a total of 104 present at the tournament – a staggering 42 per cent – graduated to top international level.

The tournament has further expanded with the addition of northern hemisphere Unions active at Under 21 level and the Pacific Islands of Fiji, Samoa and Tonga, giving it a global dimension. The logical decision of the IRB to add it to its portfolio of world events has been as welcome as it has been overdue. The original four participants have had automatic entry, with a further eight gaining their right to play through their respective regional competitions. The top five in the Six Nations (this year France, Wales, England, Ireland and Italy), the winner of the Europe continental competition (Romania), Japan from Asia, and Fiji representing the Pacific Islands completed the 12-strong field in 2002. Irrespective of their standards, expectations and achievements, the overall feeling, from bottom-placed Romania to the winners, was that the competition had been a tremendous success. 'Everybody has benefited from this tournament – players and management. We were all under extreme pressure with games so close to each other. However, it was a great learning curve,' said England coach Brian Ashton.

South Africa Under 21 managed to rekindle memories of the 1995 RWC fairy tale with a remarkable string of performances against teams of nominally superior pedigree and higher expectations – New Zealand and Australia, in particular. The young Boks, led by their inspirational captain, Clyde Rathbone, beat New Zealand 19-18 in a dramatic semi-final clash and finally prevailed 24-21 over the Australians in the last match of the tournament, both teams contributing to a magnificent rugby spectacle, which had drama, excitement, skill and poetry. 'In the future, all Unions will concentrate their elite efforts on two international teams: the Test side and the Under 21s, and in this respect the Under 21 World Cup is a very important and necessary stepping stone for world rugby,' French manager Jean-Claude Skrela concluded.

# REVIEW OF THE
# SEASON 2001-02

# State of the Unions
## Where to Now for the Six Nations?

by CHRIS JONES

'The emergence of many talented players in France and England has only confirmed the view that the championship is now in three parts. The upper level is occupied by those two major countries; the middle ground is where Ireland are very comfortable, and they are joined by Wales and Scotland; while Italy occupy the bottom level and are in danger of disappearing into the cellar unless they fast-track new players.'

The evolution of the Six Nations Championship will reach a critical stage this season with the return to terrestrial screens of all the matches in the most exciting northern hemisphere rugby tournament. England's deal with Sky is over, and while the many millions the company pumped into English rugby helped give life to the fledgling professional game, the lack of exposure – the biggest games at Twickenham barely brought in one million viewers – hurt the sport. Now the BBC along with the other contracted host broadcasters around Europe will give rugby a marvellous shop window in World Cup year, and maybe, just maybe, we can start to arrest the annual drain of players from the game.

It is impossible to quantify what damage (yes, it's a harsh, but fair, verdict) has been done to the sport by the disappearance of England's home games from the majority of the nation's television screens. Only a fool would claim that the satellite deal did not hamper the sport's development at a time of outstanding English domination of the championship, during which England fell three times at the last Grand Slam hurdle. Now English fallibility will be there for all to see instead of being reduced to highlights on news packages or witnessed at the local pub/club.

This increased accessibility of the Six Nations Championship comes in the build-up to the 2003 Rugby World Cup in Australia, and if a northern hemisphere country – well, France or England! – is going to halt the southern hemisphere domination of the Webb Ellis Trophy, then a 2003 Grand Slam campaign is a must.

To win the World Cup you have to put together a run of consistent form, and the same is true of the Six Nations Championship. France were the best team last season, won all their matches, picked up the Grand Slam and proved they could be a threat in Australia. England lost in Paris to continue the whispering campaign in the game that they just cannot win when it really matters. One-off triumphs in the autumn internationals at Twickenham are something of an English speciality, but England have consistently come up one match short of a full house in the championship when playing away (Dublin, Wembley, Murrayfield and Paris), and that does not bode well for a World Cup challenge Down Under.

Despite the new £65 million BBC deal for the Six Nations rights, this year's championship will, effectively, be over after the first round of matches when England take on France at Twickenham. It amazes those who sell television rights that the Six Nations does not ring-fence that fixture and ensure it takes place on the final weekend.

Of course, that is amazingly presumptuous and suggests that only England or France can possibly win the championship and Grand Slam. Irish, Welsh, Scottish and Italian supporters would be up in arms if the England-France fixture was always tagged onto the end of the schedule, but is the idea really that outlandish?

Except for the occasional foray into true world class by Keith Wood's Ireland team, the Six Nations has, effectively, become a battle between just two nations – England and France. Now that professionalism has started to take hold, both of these rugby countries are starting to reap a tangible benefit from their huge playing bases.

In previous decades, youngsters with rugby talent would be missed because the scouting system was haphazard. Now there are academies attached to every professional outfit and they search out the potential stars of the future with real intensity because, just as football has discovered, you have to breed your own players if costly transfer dealings are to be avoided.

Last season saw the emergence of new talent in the French and English squads, and the Six Nations is an outstanding arena to discover if that potential can be realised at the very highest level of the game. Competition for places drives a squad to greater things, and that was certainly the case with France in last season's championship.

England travelled to Argentina last summer with a squad that had so many well-known faces missing it struggled to warrant the tag of 'second choice'. It was expected that the improving Pumas on their home soil would defeat England just as they had lowered the colours of Grand Slam champions France a week earlier.

Overconfidence and the emergence of new stars in England jerseys allowed head coach Clive Woodward to wear the smile of man who had walked out of his Buenos Aires hotel without his wallet and picked up a huge wad of money in the street. England had expected the one-off international to be a screen test for just one man – Charlie Hodgson, the Sale outside half, who is the back-up to Jonny Wilkinson.

Instead, men like Joe Worsley, Lewis Moody, the outstanding Ben Kay and wing Phil Christophers grabbed the limelight with Hodgson, and Woodward will go into this Six Nations Championship with the real option of leaving Lions captain Martin Johnson and flanker Neil Back out of the starting line-up. While this may strike many as a ridiculous idea – given the experience of Johnson and Back – the game is moving forward so quickly that a saying used by former England and Lions manager Geoff Cooke is very appropriate: 'The graveyard is full of indispensable men'.

Champions France have also undertaken root and branch work within their squad, and coach Bernard Laporte has shown a willingness to give youth a chance at the highest level. The emergence of outstanding centre Damien Traille, No. 8 Imanol Harinordoquy and outside half Gérald Merceron plus the new life breathed into captain Fabien Galthié have given the French a cutting edge that they lacked for too many seasons.

*BELOW* Fabien Galthié feeds Gérald Merceron as back-rowers Olivier Magne (right) and Imanol Harinordoquy look on in France's 20-15 win over England.

*BELOW RIGHT* World-class talent Brian O'Driscoll leaves Mauro Bergamasco clutching thin air at Lansdowne Road as Italy suffer yet another defeat, 32-17.

There is also the return to fitness of Thomas Castaignède, at Saracens, to offer France another attacking option, one that still has a special place in the hearts of French supporters. Additionally, the ability to get the ball wide quickly is a real strength in the French game because flankers Olivier Magne and Serge Betsen have become a potent combination either side of young Harinordoquy.

The emergence of many talented players in France and England has only confirmed the view that the championship is now in three parts. The upper level is occupied by those two major countries; the middle ground is where Ireland are very comfortable, and they are joined by Wales and Scotland; while Italy occupy the bottom level and are in danger of disappearing into the cellar unless they fast-track new players.

Ireland and Wales have had to deal with the disruption caused by a change of coaching structure and playing numbers that offers only a certain amount of flexibility. The Irish, led by Wood, are always a problem at home but lose their focus away from Lansdowne Road. Despite the presence of the brilliant Brian O'Driscoll at centre, they are still looking for the right balance in midfield to bring out the best in this special talent.

Up front, the Irish are still ultra-competitive and will relish the chance of ruining another English Grand Slam bid – if that is how things work out – in the final round of this season's championship matches. In many ways, the Ireland v England game will be a match that sets the tone for England's World Cup challenge, as they follow a trip to Dublin with Tests in New Zealand and Australia next summer. Outside the World Cup itself there can be no greater test of their ability to win away from home.

# saracens | foundation

enhancing the lives of young people through sport

This national and regional award-winning programme of work is making a real difference for young people - **why don't you get involved too?**

Just call **01923 204605** for information on how you can help.

Registered Charity Number 1079316

Wales and Scotland took part in one of the worst championship matches in years in Cardiff last season. It was an awful advert for the Six Nations and we can only hope that the fitness and skills work put in during the close season pays off in the competition because that is the only way the ever-increasing gulf in consistency is going to be addressed.

The Scots have expanded their domestic playing options with the new Borders team, while Wales have once again failed to deal with calls for a smaller number of top clubs to concentrate the very best players. Two Welsh forwards have been told they will not be picked until their fitness levels reach international standards, and it is amazing that they need this kind of 'big stick' threat to play at the highest level of the game. However, it just highlights that something fundamental is still missing from the domestic game in Wales.

For Italy, the problems are huge. They have attempted to address the lack of playing depth by raiding the best young talent in Argentina and these useful arrivals will force their way into the national squad in the next two or three years. In the meantime, it's a case of trying to find a win – any win – to go with their only success to date, against Scotland.

Reports that Italy could be thrown out of the Six Nations were dismissed out of hand by the organisers, and that vote of confidence was needed. Rome has been a hugely successful addition to the away trip schedule for all supporters, but the delights of the city would be even greater if they included a truly competitive rugby team. It's what the Six Nations needs and television audiences will demand in 2003.

**ABOVE** Rob Howley, in his last international match, runs at the Leslie brothers during the disappointing Wales v Scotland game at Cardiff, which ended in a 27-22 victory for the Scots.

# The Club Scene
## England: Now Europe's Best Clubs?

by **BILL MITCHELL**

'The idea of the play-offs, which might be a success if they were to be held at the start of a new season, is to pitch the eight best teams in the league into an ultimate trial of strength.'

This was another highly successful season for English clubs, with the European 'double' achieved once again courtesy of Leicester retaining the Heineken Cup by beating Munster at the Millennium Stadium in Cardiff and Sale taking the Parker Pen Shield after a thrilling encounter against Welsh Principality Cup winners Pontypridd at Oxford's Kassam Stadium. Leicester also recorded yet another Zurich Premiership success, a league triumph that was predictable almost from the start of the campaign. This effectively did not come to life until the European preliminaries had been completed, and Leicester's final margin of victory in the competition was a massive 14 points from Sale, with Gloucester a point further away. But neither could claim that they had given the Tigers a realistic challenge.

Leicester's European success would have been written off as coming up to routine expectations had the match against Munster not ended on an unnecessarily controversial note. Their high-profile flanker Neil Back, always a superb and wholehearted player, committed an offence at a scrum out of sight of the referee, which could have brought him a yellow card and given the Irishmen a penalty close to the line. It was plain cheating and for anyone to condone it is quite sickening and adds nothing to the prestige of a game that can do without bad publicity.

There is an appropriate noun that describes people who are seen to cheat, and no one who does so can complain if it is used against them – or are we all being naive if we hope to see today's role models set a good example to the game's aficionados? That was the second serious incident

involving Leicester during the season, which was very sad to see coming from Europe's best club. They are far too good and well organised to need to resort to skulduggery for victories.

Another discussion point concerned the foot of the table, which was eventually occupied by Leeds after a late 'dog fight' also involving Bath, Saracens and Harlequins. None of these sides were relegated because a commission of enquiry effectively ruled out Rotherham, the National First Division champions, because their ground arrangements for the 2002-03 season had not been properly completed before a deadline set for the end of March 2002. Any fair-minded person would endorse this decision as being reasonable according to the accepted competition rules – but for one anomaly, which concerned Wasps, whose own plans for a move of ground to High Wycombe had not been settled at the time the Rotherham decision was announced. One law for the rich and one for the poor? Also, some people felt that to keep interest in the final matches alive the decision had been kept under wraps longer than was necessary.

**ABOVE** Heath celebrate after defeating Bromley 16-10 in the Powergen Junior Cup.

**LEFT** Freddie Tuilagi crosses for Leicester Tigers as they clinch the 2001-02 Premiership, defeating Newcastle Falcons 20-12 at Welford Road.

Leicester once again failed to win the knockout trophy (the Powergen Cup) after once more falling victim to Harlequins at the Stoop Memorial Ground, this time at the quarter-final stage by a narrow 22-20 scoreline. Their conquerors then only just lost (27-32) in their home semi-final against London Irish, while Northampton in their last-four encounter with Newcastle had won the match by half-time, the eventual 38-7 scoreline giving the impression that they might start the Twickenham final as favourites.

As it happened, the same score was recorded in the final, but it was London Irish (very few of whose players are actually Irish) who were on the right end of that result, with once again the outcome seeming inevitable before the teams went inside to have their half-time cups of

tea – or whatever. The most significant points about the afternoon were the attendance of 73,000 and the fact that the paying spectators had been accorded a quadruple bill with good matches being provided in the Junior Cup final, won 16-10 by Heath against Bromley; the Intermediate Cup final, a comfortable 43-19 victory for Halifax over Gosport & Fareham; and in the final of a new competition for non-Premiership clubs, the Challenge Shield, which went the way of Rotherham against gallant Exeter (35-26). It was a great day for Yorkshire apart from the main event. The formula of a day of finals has been a big success for seven years in Scotland, where three such matches take place on a day in late April. One's only concern is whether the ground, however well maintained, can take the pressure, but the public must love it and that is what matters. A great idea!

In contrast the Zurich Premiership play-offs were, to be truthful, non-events, as the attendance of 28,500 at the Twickenham final, played as late as 8 June, must testify. The organisers must have been relieved that the crowd was not even smaller, as it might have been had West Country rivals Bristol and Gloucester not been the finalists. The idea of the play-offs, which might be a success if they were to be held at the start of a new season, is to pitch the eight best teams in the league into an ultimate trial of strength. But the event was burdened by a number of factors and distractions apart from the lateness in the season of the programme. Both Leicester and Sale had European finals, which had to take priority over this competition, while London Irish showed their interest by fielding a second string in their quarter-final defeat against their earlier Twickenham victors, Northampton.

**ABOVE** Gloucester, with captain Phil Vickery in the thick of things, get the partying under way after beating Bristol Shoguns 28-23 at HQ to win the Zurich Championship.

**RIGHT** Jonah Lomu is tackled by back-rower James Forrester as the Barbarians go down to England at Twickenham by 53 points to 29.

The whole thing is possibly meant to bring in more money to the top clubs – and heaven knows that nearly all of them have anxious bank managers breathing down their necks – but this is clearly not a way to achieve that objective. In fact, the lack of sufficient funds despite generous sponsorship deals is a semi-permanent feature of the real professional end of the game. But would not the clubs fare better if they did not have such expensive playing staffs, a problem that RFU regulations, well intentioned though they are, have failed to solve? Financial disputes involving strife with the RFU are never far away and have not been since the game turned professional. Do the top clubs want too much for themselves?

However, rugby in England is not the preserve of the top outfits and there was plenty of good competition lower down the scale. Rotherham beat Worcester, who must soon be realistic contenders for higher status, in a tough battle for National League first division honours, while Bracknell, Henley and Manchester at the wrong end of the table were slightly outclassed but never disgraced. Orrell and Plymouth Albion slogged it out for the second division title, with the former, only recently among the leading English clubs, edging out their rivals only on points difference. Sedgley Park are to be commended for staying in contention for most of the season, but at the foot of the division it was sad to see such famous clubs as Preston Grasshoppers and Waterloo struggling to gain any points at all.

The two National third divisions showed that an ambitious club does not need a reputation before challenging for better things. In the North, Doncaster along with midlanders Dudley Kingswinford were excellent examples of this, while the South became a Cornish monopoly with Penzance & Newlyn beating Launceston by a short head (one point) for the title.

Every piece of silver lining has a cloud, and the demises of Sandal and the recently high-profile West Hartlepool in the North along with Clifton and Cinderford in the South are sad to see. One can only wish them better fortunes in the future, but it will be a tough road back for them all. The replacements, six in number, include two (Havant and Weston-super-Mare) who were there before and four new names – Broadstreet from the Midlands, Basingstoke from the South and two Yorkshire clubs in Halifax and Hull Ionians. All are ambitious and will be a problem for established sides.

Outside the league competitions it was again good to see the Barbarians flourishing, as all the game's lovers wish to see happen, their season bringing four wins from six matches. Defeats at the hands of Australia and England (a superb 53-29 victory at Twickenham) were countered by excellent performances against Combined Services, East Midlands, Wales and Scotland. If they are an anachronism, may we have more of the kind!

The Army regained the services honours from the Navy as a result of an easy success against the Royal Air Force, who are struggling at the moment, and a dour Twickenham win against the sailors. However, the new five-team tournament involving the three services and Oxford and Cambridge Universities went to the Isis men as a result of their Varsity Match win, when for once a poor contest was witnessed after several good games recently. It may be a good time for the captains for the new season – both New Zealanders – to have a lunch together as Roy Allaway and John Clements did in 1955 and aim to reward the usual big crowd with a classic encounter, which was the outcome of that earlier meeting. The crowds will not continue to be so good if we have another near stalemate.

The BUSA final – also at Twickenham – made up in many ways for the joyless Varsity event. It was a thriller won 25-23 by Brunel West London against St Mary's University College, whose Hallett missed a difficult injury-time conversion attempt that would have brought the scores level. The County Championship was revamped for this season, after the ravages of foot-and-mouth last campaign, so that the lesser sides had a small competition of their own. The main final was again played at Headquarters and resulted in a very close struggle between Gloucestershire and Cheshire, who had qualified courtesy of a tries countback after a 37-37 draw with Yorkshire. Their luck did not hold, and the West Country lads won narrowly (26-23), with Warwickshire taking the consolation shield competition final 34-12 against Berkshire.

Nowadays, sevens tournaments in England are fairly low-key affairs, with the Middlesex Charity event being held at Twickenham in August. The Army were the latest winners, fielding an impressive array of Fijians, who were just too good for Newcastle in the final. Further afield, who can forget the brilliant England VII who won the Hong Kong Sevens for the first time since the 1980s? In sevens, though, it is the schools events that hold sway, and the Rosslyn Park Sevens competition, superbly organised by the club and the Tanner family and sponsored by the Army recently, is the yardstick by which most schools measure their season's achievements.

A season from any country's point of view is assessed according to how the national team has fared. In this respect England did well against the touring sides but failed yet again to win a Grand Slam in the disrupted 2001 Six Nations and then finished second in the 2002 competition. However, manager Clive Woodward did neither the team nor the integrity of the game of rugby any favours by insisting on playing Martin Johnson (and as captain, too) for the game against France, when Johnson was under a very heavy cloud after a serious incident early in the year. It seemed that it was the intention of the management to play Johnson, whose previous indiscipline on the field is well documented, in any circumstances, and his availability had only been made possible through delaying tactics over an appeal against suspension.

At times, and most unjustly in the majority of cases, England teams have had to contend with paranoid unpopularity from other nations' fans. On this occasion, though, the disgust at such a poor example set by the England management was understandable, as Johnson had been guilty of a violent assault against the Saracens hooker Robin Russell at Watford on 9 February. Russell sustained a nasty facial injury as a result, and Johnson was extremely fortunate to be given only a yellow card (as was his unlucky victim, later officially rescinded on RFU instructions) by referee Pearson, who, along with his touch judges, had not seen the incident.

In any properly run sport some kind of disciplinary action was absolutely necessary, given the fact that damning video evidence had been seen nationally and was still available. Robert Horner, the RFU disciplinary officer, showed great courage in refusing to be browbeaten into dropping the charge. A three-week suspension was decreed. One appeal upheld the sentence, which would have made Johnson unavailable for Paris, but a further plea was lodged, which made him available. So an otherwise inspiring captain took the field in highly contentious circumstances.

By now both player and club seemed to be confident that further entreaties would see Johnson avoid any penalty. Another appeal session was convened, at which an Oxford law don, David Pannick, presided. After another lengthy series of spurious arguments (double jeopardy, etc) put forward by an expensive team of lawyers, the pleadings were dismissed. Common sense had prevailed and Johnson had to serve a suspension, which meant that he missed the Twickenham game against Wales. By an irony, when he was free again he was picked only for the bench by Woodward for the Italy game, although he eventually did appear as a replacement. Many good things emerged from this shoddy affair, among them the lesson that no player or club, however famous, is above the law. At the same time the RFU realised that disciplinary matters should be streamlined so that such cynical acts of procrastination could not recur.

Looking forward, though, the new season promises to be one great thrill, and with a World Cup in Australia coming along at the end of the year everyone will be on their toes. Will anyone dethrone champions Leicester? Can England finally achieve that elusive Grand Slam after four consecutive one-match failures? Floreat rugby!

# Scotland: Hawick at the Double

### by ALAN LORIMER

'The talented youngsters in the system might take their labour elsewhere, and at a time when national coach Ian McGeechan is advocating a stay-at-home policy, such migration would be undesirable.'

It was the future rather than the past that created excitement in Scottish professional club rugby last season with the creation of a third district side. It represented an increase of 50 per cent in the number of professional clubs and was a move, it is hoped by the faithful north of the border, which will lead to a richer pool of talent to supply the national teams. Such growth is certainly needed. Scotland's failings at international level have been attributed in part to the lack of competition for places in both the senior and A teams and in part to a lack of overall numbers. Enter Scotland's third team, based at Netherdale in Galashiels and unambiguously named The Borders.

Headed by the former All Black assistant coach Tony Gilbert, The Borders have attracted back to Scotland a number of high-profile players, who include the enigmatic Gregor Townsend, himself a Galashiels product, and the doyen scrum half Gary Armstrong. The talent is there. What remains to be answered is the effectiveness of the new outfit. But at least those playing for The Borders will not have to undergo the draining fortnightly bus journey to Wales, following the decision taken at the end of last season to discontinue the Welsh/Scottish League.

The abandonment of this particular alliance leaves Scotland's three professional sides with a slimmed-down competitive programme and the answer, maybe, to player burn-out. It may have been hated and even derided by some of the players, but the Welsh/Scottish League served its purpose by exposing Scotland's nascent professional scene to the realities of rugby life. Away matches against the likes of Pontypridd or Bridgend were sufficient to acquaint Scotland's pros with the school of hard knocks.

Of the two Scottish sides in the Welsh/Scottish League last season, it was Edinburgh who fared the better, finishing in sixth position, two places above Glasgow. Edinburgh's record of ten wins, eight defeats and two draws from their 20 games tells the tale of inconsistency, or rather of the inability to perform well away from home, as the 36-3 defeat by Neath at the Gnoll illustrates so clearly. Was it those bus journeys? Or was it a lack of real professionalism? Or maybe it was the absence of a high-profile player. That problem, however, was solved when Edinburgh signed the former New Zealand captain Todd Blackadder along with the Otago utility back Brendan Laney.

The pre-Christmas arrival of Blackadder (representing a break from the stated policy of playing only Scotland-qualified players) had a massive effect on the Edinburgh side, the famous All Black reputedly taking over much of the coaching and tactical thinking within the capital team. Laney, meanwhile, had hardly stepped off the plane from New Zealand than he was wearing the Scotland full back jersey – at the expense of his Edinburgh clubmate Derrick Lee, who a week earlier had

been named player of the match against Argentina after an exhilarating performance in which he scored the Scots' only try.

Part of Edinburgh's inconsistency may also have been due to the management's inability to settle the stand-off tussle between Duncan Hodge and Gordon Ross. In the event an alternating policy ensued, and with it a loss of confidence by both players. Ultimately Hodge was the preferred choice at national level as the back-up to Gregor Townsend, and this was reflected in the Edinburgh side, leaving Ross redundant for much of the second half of the season. Meanwhile, Calvin Howarth, the third stand-off in the Edinburgh squad, was all but ignored until he was sensibly transferred, or loaned as it was officially termed, to Glasgow. Among the forwards, props Craig Smith and Allan Jacobsen advanced their claims for promotion, lock Nathan Hines made a significant return after injury and in the back row Andrew Dall clearly benefited from the guidance of Blackadder.

Outwith the Welsh/Scottish League, Edinburgh disappointed in both the Heineken European Cup and the Celtic League. Drawn alongside Bath, Biarritz and Swansea, Edinburgh achieved only one win – against Swansea – in a lukewarm campaign. In the early-season Celtic competition, Edinburgh were equally unimpressive, finishing sixth out of seven with just two victories – over Connacht and Caerphilly.

Fifty miles to the west the story was much the same, despite a strong start by Glasgow in the Celtic League. While Edinburgh foundered miserably in this competition, Glasgow progressed to the knockout stages, defeating Connacht away in the quarter-finals before losing to Leinster in the semis. At European level, Glasgow earned credit by coming close to qualifying for the later stages of the Heineken Cup. Glasgow were unbeaten at home – they inflicted defeats on Cardiff and Northampton Saints, but the 19-19 draw against Montferrand proved costly. But as in other competitions it was Glasgow's inability to make a dent in the opposition away from home that was the real reason for their failure to go beyond the pool stages. Glasgow's eighth place in the Welsh/Scottish League marked another disappointment for coach Richie Dixon's side, the away record being particularly dismal both in terms of results and margins of defeat.

On the positive side, Glasgow began to attract sizeable crowds for their home matches at Hughenden and could take further satisfaction from the progress of some of their younger players. Of these, centre Andrew Henderson figured in the Scotland side, while winger Rory Kerr impressed for Scotland A and deservedly won a place on the Scots' tour of North America.

At times both professional club sides were forced by injury problems to 'borrow' players from amateur teams. But at least the call-up of so-called amateurs and their subsequent ability to perform well showed that the talent is there in the non-professional side of the game.

*ABOVE LEFT* Glasgow centre Andrew Henderson, flanked by Tommy Hayes (left) and James McLaren, lines up his opposite number.

*RIGHT* Hawick captain Kevin Reid has his kick charged down by Euan Murray of Glasgow Hawks during the 2002 BT Cellnet Cup final, which Hawick won 20-17.

Certainly the BT Scotland Premiership still makes good viewing even without the star names in Scotland rugby, and the average age of the competition's players has gone down following the exodus of the current crop of pros.

Watching the Premiership was watching the next generation of professional players, especially if you happened to be a regular visitor to Mansfield Park, where Hawick had a rich crop of talent. At the end of last season, four of Hawick's championship-winning team were signed for The Borders – winger Nikki Walker, centre Stephen Cranston, lock Scott MacLeod and prop Craig Dunlea.

Hawick had begun last season as defending champions and were determined to maintain their grip on the title. Their main challengers were Boroughmuir, and in the event the championship became a two-horse race as Melrose and Heriot's fell off the pace. The crunch game between the two principals became the meeting at Mansfield Park, but what should have been a showcase match was ruined by the appalling conditions. This reinforced the view widely held by players and coaches, if not gaining huge popularity among committee men, that rugby should be a non-winter sport. An injury-time goal by Hawick's stand-off Neil Stenhouse gave the Greens a 25-22 win, and from then on Hawick kept their nerve, winning all their remaining matches to finish one point ahead of Boroughmuir for a second successive title. Hawick's achievement was all the more creditable as it followed an internal row that resulted in the resignation of coach Ian Barnes. Former Scotland scrum half Greg Oliver took over and successfully guided the 'Green Machine' to their goal.

Only one team, Melrose, had previously achieved a league and cup double. Hawick, winners of the cup in its inaugural year, coveted the trophy and achieved their ambition, winning the BT Cellnet Cup at Murrayfield with a 20-17 victory in a thrilling final against past winners Glasgow Hawks that went to extra time. For Hawks, their appearance in the final at Murrayfield was

consolation for their disappointing showing in the Premiership, where a poor start to the season cost them dearly. Hawks certainly had talented players in Under 19 centre Tom Philip, half backs Stephen Duffy and Kenny Sinclair and forwards Rory Mackay and Richard Maxton.

Elsewhere in the Premiership, the fourth-place finish of newcomers Aberdeen GSFP struck a blow for devolution and raised genuine hope that rugby in the northeast of Scotland can flourish on the back of Grammar's success. To an extent it already has, with Ellon now regularly producing top players and showing their team strength by winning the BT Cellnet Bowl final at Murrayfield.

In a fiercely contested Premiership the losers were Kirkcaldy, whose two-year tenure in the first division was doomed early on in the season after a succession of defeats, and Gala, who lost out to Stirling County in the struggle to stay in the top tier. Borders rugby may have lost Gala from the first division, but the gain through the promotion of Peebles and Jed-Forest compensated and reinforced the view that club rugby's centre of gravity is still in the south of Scotland. The rise of Peebles was the most interesting phenomenon in Scottish club rugby and very much down to the form of their former Melrose player-coach Scott Nichol, who last season played the best rugby of his long career. Lower down the divisions, Dunfermline, having regrouped over the past few seasons, were promoted from the National Leagues, while Stirling University proved that student rugby is prospering by climbing to the fourth division.

Looking at amateur club rugby overall, the impression is that the top end is still under-performing despite the young talent in the first division clubs. A number of ideas have been floated, including that of ensuring best practice by central funding of coaches. It seems that semi-professionalism may have to be officially introduced to the top layer of the Premiership, which, after all, should be the interface between the amateur and professional games. Otherwise, it is argued, the talented youngsters in the system might take their labour elsewhere, and at a time when national coach Ian McGeechan is advocating a stay-at-home policy, such migration would be undesirable.

**BELOW** Kirkcaldy gained some consolation for dropping out of the Scottish Premiership first division by winning the BT Cellnet Shield, beating Stewartry 41-12 in the final.

# Wales: A Question of Money?

## by DAVID STEWART

'Standards on the field are slowly improving, partly due to the increased professionalism and skill levels of young players coming through. The challenge for the Welsh game is to achieve the correct structure.'

'**M**oney, it's a crime,' sang Pink Floyd all those years ago. Well, the Welsh club scene continues to change in structure, much of the change driven by the difficulties of financing the professional game. Llanelli were the last winners of the Welsh/Scottish League, the competition being discontinued – at least as far as Scots participation is concerned; they don't bring anything much by way of a travelling support, you see, so gate receipts are adversely affected. An EGM of the Union was held to debate a proposal, promoted by director of rugby Terry Cobner and supported by former national coach Graham Henry, to reduce the number of premier clubs from nine to six; the motion was defeated. The official rationale for the proposal was that there isn't enough talent around to cover the larger number of sides; the unofficial one was that the Union's money distribution to the 'elite' would go 50 per cent further if three clubs were cut adrift. Neath have already been purchased by the Union to avoid closure, Llanelli's ground was previously bought by the Union in a bail-out exercise, Swansea and Pontypridd needed financial help last term, and in the close season it looked like Ebbw Vale's Steelmen might follow the town's famous steelworks into oblivion.

An offshoot of the finance issue is that qualification for the Heineken Cup has become something of a Holy Grail, such is the remuneration from that competition. Winning it has become an understandable obsession for Llanelli coach Gareth Jenkins. Distraught is the only word which fairly sums up his countenance after Tim Stimpson's penalty kick from the Leicester half in the semi-final at Nottingham Forest had once again deprived his beloved club of a final place, which this time would have been before a 'home' crowd at the Millennium Stadium.

Jenkins could be forgiven for never wanting to play a big game in a soccer stadium again, such was the sense of déjà vu from two years earlier at Reading's Madejski, when the hand of Ian Boobyer and the boot of Paul Grayson occasioned a similar outcome. Cork-based referee David McHugh was apparently alert enough to detect Martin Madden (as opposed to his opponent Darren Garforth) 'drop' the scrum but not to see Stimpson indulge in the now-regular goal-kicker's habit of 'stealing' a few extra metres. Surely match officials should be alert to this and issue yellow cards under Law 10 – Acts contrary to good sportsmanship. Such was the discomfort Garforth was subjected to by the about-to-retire Peter Clohessy of McHugh's Munster in the final that he may have considered the ref's gift to be a dubious one. Of Neil Back's sportsmanship that day, enough has already been written elsewhere.

The Scarlets earned a decent measure of consolation by winning the league, ironically with a very late penalty goal from the outstanding Stephen Jones in their last match against Cardiff at the Arms Park. The competition had a most exciting climax, with Newport, Neath and Cardiff all in the frame as the last round of matches was played. All have qualified for the European Cup and its 'loot', along with Swansea. That is hard on Pontypridd, who in many respects were the team of the year.

A sluggish start in the new Celtic League saw Richie Collins depart as Pontypridd coach to be replaced by the estimable Lynn Howells. Not retained by Cardiff after a two-year spell, nor by Wales as Steve Hansen came in to coach the forwards, Howells returned to the homely club which

represents the town known as the Gateway to the Rhondda and proceeded not only to turn their season around in spectacular fashion but also to prove his own credentials beyond dispute, and in doing so struck a timely bow for the qualities of the domestic coach at a time when expensive southern hemisphere blow-ins are all the rage.

No sooner did the excellent Ian McIntosh leave Newport – having usurped Allan Lewis with no greater achievement in terms of winning trophies or European progress – than Swansea were replacing the ultimately unsuccessful John Plumtree with Queensland's John Connolly, late of Stade Français. How depressing that the new man then brings in another Aussie to assist. Whither the opportunity for a local coach of promise to learn from someone of 'Knuckles' experience? Wonder how the Union views that expenditure of their share of Swansea's funding? We're back again to money, but, oops, the national team are onto their second Kiwi, now assisted by Scott Johnson of Australia. People in glass houses can't stand up in the bath, can they?

*ABOVE* Llanelli's Leigh Davies brings down Lewis Moody as the Scarlets go down 13-12 to the Tigers in the Heineken semis.

*ABOVE RIGHT* Pontypridd celebrate as Mefin Davies scores in their Parker Pen semi-final victory over London Irish.

*RIGHT* Pontypridd's Dale McIntosh with the Principality Cup after Ponty's 20-17 defeat of Llanelli in the final.

Pontypridd had an outstanding conclusion to the season. Howells noted that 'We don't have the depth of squad available to other clubs, so we just keep putting our best XV on the field and hope they can keep going'. How they did just that – beating Saracens and London Irish en route to the final of the Parker Pen Shield, where they led Sale at half-time before running out of gas and going down 22-25. A week earlier, however, the 'Valley Commandos', as they like to be styled, had beaten the aristocrats from Stradey 20-17 in the Principality Cup final, to earn some much-deserved silverware. Reward for

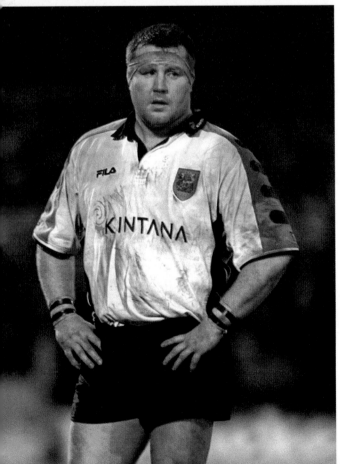

individuals saw five of their busy and organised pack selected as uncapped players for the Welsh tour of South Africa. The talented Michael Owen (there's a phrase we've heard before) became his country's 1000th capped player in the absence of injured skipper Scott Quinnell, and his team-mates Richard Parks, Mefin Davies and Robert Sidoli had run-on parts in the Tests. Few doubt that promising loose-head Gethin Jenkins will be far behind.

Cardiff had a bit of a cost-cutting clear-out after another trophyless season, with Craig Quinnell and Robert Howley heading for the Zurich Premiership. Rudi Joubert returned to the sun and Super 12 in Africa, and David Young takes over as head coach.

*ABOVE*   Craig Quinnell, seen here pursued by Budge Pountney of Northampton, is on his way from Cardiff to the Zurich Premiership.

*LEFT*   Rudi Joubert having returned to South Africa, David Young takes over as Cardiff head coach.

*RIGHT*   Swansea's Colin Charvis and Scott Gibbs bring Calvin Howarth of Edinburgh to a halt. Having retired from international rugby, Gibbs is free to concentrate his efforts on the club game.

Swansea were a bit of a mess for most of the season, a particular low point being a defeat at second division Pontypool Park in the cup, although they did rally in the latter part. Scott Gibbs' withdrawal from the international fray means he is able to concentrate his considerable firepower on club duties in the season ahead. Neath were the surprise package, with the venerable Allan Bateman and the internationally restored Gareth Llewellyn mentoring a bunch of promising youngsters under the wily and occasionally provocative coaching of Lyn Jones, and with a wage bill considerably smaller than their main rivals'. They had a good Celtic League campaign, including the scalp of the mighty Munster at the Gnoll.

That competition, though still unsponsored, proved to be a major success, and although the coming season provides only seven games for each club within two pools prior to a last-eight knockout, it is hoped that after the 2003 World Cup it can evolve into a full home-and-away situation for all competing sides. Whether in time our brethren across the Severn will wise up to the widely held belief that a British Isles league is the natural order remains to be seen. Again, finance is likely to dictate, and the interest of broadcasters and sponsors will be primary.

This column last year predicted ongoing success for Cardiff and Swansea last term – no clairvoyance there, then! Still, let's be bold and predict well-resourced (courtesy of a high-profile chairman) Bridgend as dark horses in the year ahead, with a contented Allan Lewis now installed as director of rugby. If their rather ordinary front five, now bolstered by second-row Andy Moore, can provide a consistent platform, their attack, with the likes of Dafydd James and Gareth Thomas, is as potent as any. Standards on the field are slowly improving, partly due to the increased professionalism and skill levels of young players coming through. The challenge for the Welsh game is to achieve the correct structure – in terms of finance, number of premier clubs and standard of competition – to establish a solvent and vibrant club scene, ultimately translating into a resurgent national one.

Well, silk on one side, pure cotton on the other to be precise. And that's on t
including the ergonomically proven "Z" position for sleeping, it extends to a f
slumber. With a host of other features such as a personal water bottle holder, priv

Be as comfortable on the ground
as you are in the air.

(Make sure the pillows you have on the ground are silk.)

NEW BUSINESS CLASS

**Asia** Miles

our new seat. Superbly designed to offer an infinite number of comfort settings
ngth of 6'3" and is "cocooned" in a hard shell to provide you with uninterrupted
reen and individual reading light, where on earth could you be so comfortable?

Now you're really flying.

# Ireland: Leinster and Shannon Clean Up

by **SEAN DIFFLEY**

'And if Munster failed at the final hurdle for the second time in three years, they still had much reason to be proud of their achievements, and their remarkable supporters, who have followed them through thick and thin, carved a special niche.'

It was one of Ireland's better seasons – from the international campaign, the Heineken European Cup and the Celtic League to the re-emergence of Shannon to take the All Ireland League club title. And if Munster failed at the final hurdle for the second time in three years, they still had much reason to be proud of their achievements, and their remarkable supporters, who have followed them through thick and thin, carved a special niche. This remarkable 'Red Army' contributed hugely towards filling Cardiff's Millennium Stadium for the final with Leicester and were not only a support to the Munster team but also a tremendous fillip to the competition that has become such a feature of the modern European game.

*BELOW LEFT* David Wallace of Munster runs at Leicester's Austin Healey during the Heineken European Cup final at the Millennium Stadium, Cardiff, which the Tigers won 15-9.

*BELOW* Rob Henderson and Jim Williams grab Leinster's Shane Horgan, but Munster were on the receiving end again in the final of the Celtic League Cup, which Leinster won 24-20.

Of course it was a great disappointment for Munster and for such stalwarts as Peter Clohessy and Mick Galwey playing in their last European Cup. But Munster were realistic enough to admit that they lost to the better team on the day. Regrettably, though, there was a sour note with Neil Back's illegal handling of the ball in that late scrum under the Leicester posts. Sure, it's history now, but Back's comment that 'I did what I had to do' and Dean Richards' remark that 'there was a lot of cheating on both sides' were not exactly greeted with a standing ovation on the other side of the Irish Sea.

Some in Munster wondered whether had Back's sleight of hand been observed by the referee and had Back had been sin-binned would Munster have managed to take advantage against seven Leicester forwards at that late stage and snatch victory. Well, it's a debating point. What is hardly a debating point is that Leicester's win was slightly tainted. Professionalism should not tarnish the old decencies of the game.

In the new season, Munster will not only be without such stalwarts as Clohessy and Galwey – the coaching staff has changed too. The quiet man, Declan Kidney, who so astutely fostered Munster's fortunes in their Heineken Cup campaigns has moved on to pastures new, becoming assistant to Irish coach Eddie O'Sullivan; Kidney's Munster assistant, Niall O'Donovan, whose prime responsibility was the Munster forwards, now becomes an assistant/forwards coach to the Irish squad.

The new Munster coach is Alan Gaffney, who was assistant to Matt Williams at Leinster. With Gaffney gone south, the new assistant to Williams in Dublin is Willie Anderson. Last season Leinster won not only the Celtic League with a renewal of something like the old mix of spirit and skill but also the Irish Inter-Provincial Championship. There were rumours at the end of the season that their charismatic Australian coach, the very popular Williams, was being offered inducements to depart, but he has renewed his contract with Leinster and expects some good results this coming season in the Celtic League and the European Cup.

In the All Ireland League for clubs the trophy returned to Limerick, the incredible Shannon winning their fifth title in a competition that began in 1995. In the 15-game campaign it was Cork Constitution who headed the table with 52 points – a point clear of Shannon, and with only two losses to Shannon's three – but following the format that has applied over the past couple of years the four top clubs play off

**ABOVE** Leinster coach Matt Williams with his children and the Celtic League Cup after the final at Lansdowne Road in December 2001. The popular Williams has renewed his contract at Leinster.

**RIGHT** The Shannon team celebrate after beating Cork Constitution 21-17 in the final of the AIB League Cup.

in semi-finals in a bid to qualify for the final. The top four were Cork Constitution, Shannon, Clontarf – the only non-Munster side – and Garryowen, and the finalists at Lansdowne Road were Con, who beat Garryowen, and Shannon, who overcame Clontarf.

Shannon won the final 21-17, going 13-0 up early in the match. For Constitution it was not quite the ordeal of the previous year, when they were hammered in the final by Dungannon, but once again the absence of Ronan O'Gara – the call of other duties – didn't help. For Shannon came two good tries by back-row Colm McMahon and wing John Lacey, one converted by Tommy Cregan, who also kicked two penalty goals. Joe Sheahan and John Kelly scored tries for Con, and Brian O'Meara converted both and kicked a penalty goal. Their great comeback failed, but in the end it was only a late, cheeky dropped goal by Shannon out-half Niall McNamara that separated the sides.

An interesting development was the victory of Belfast Harlequins in the final of division two of the league; they beat UL Bohemians from Limerick 43-29. Thus Harlequins – an amalgam of NIFC and Collegians, famous clubs of the past – are now in the top division and should create problems for the very best. Harlequins' try tally for the season in 13 matches was 85 and they finished 18 points ahead of the rest in the league table. Between them this past season, the backs – John Lowe, Rhys Botha, Ajay Derwin, Andy Lowe, Sheldon Coulter, Niall Malone and Andy Park – managed just over 50 tries between them.

The business of the top four playing off for the league title took a strange twist in division three. The top four in the third division were Greystones, Dublin University, Old Wesley and Connemara. That meant that Greystones and Dublin University were promoted. Yet while Dublin University beat Old Wesley in their semi-final play-off, Greystones lost to Connemara. Then came the great irony at Lansdowne Road, when all divisional finals took place on the same Saturday afternoon. In the division three final Connemara, from the town of Clifden, way out near the Atlantic coastline, won the final, beating Dublin University 25-21. Yet Connemara will remain in division three next season. This will add to the ongoing debate as to whether the system is the right one. The winners of the final stay put, but two others go up to the higher division.

# France: Biarritz's Recipe for Success

## by CHRIS THAU

'But Biarritz's victory is probably more important than that, because the club's approach to success may offer French – and not only French – rugby a model for the future.'

The fact that Biarritz Olympique won the 101st French Championship title last June is probably more significant than certain sections of French rugby would be prepared to admit. To some of the traditionalists, the Biarritz v Agen clash in the final was about right and wrong, about fair and foul play, and ultimately about the soul of French rugby. This may sound a bit melodramatic, but it is true to an extent. To others it was just another rugby encounter, though somewhat tainted by the way one of the participants, Agen, had chosen to lose a highly controversial match in the European Shield. But whatever your point of view, it was after all the 2002 French Championship final, and it had a fairy-tale ending.

Biarritz are your average French club, sustained by moderate funding and with a modest supporter base. Since their heyday in the mid- and late 1930s, when they won the Bouclier de Brennus twice – in 1935 and 1939 – in four appearances in the final, Biarritz's forays to the forefront of French rugby have been fairly infrequent. They featured in the final of the 1992 French Championship, losing to the new-look Toulon in the match that was Serge Blanco's final farewell.

On the other hand, Agen, the celebrated club of former presidents Batigne and Ferrasse, have been the 'establishment club' for decades, with 12 appearances in the final and eight championship titles under their belt. The days when a player had to play for Agen to be considered for France are long gone, but the feeling that Agen can do with impunity certain things for which other clubs would be severely punished still lingers on.

The debate about Agen's cynical 'dereliction of duty' against the Welsh club Ebbw Vale in the European Parker Pen Shield, which resulted in the club's suspension from European competition for a year, has been rumbling on in French rugby. Agen have never accepted responsibility, let alone apologised, for their conduct. The vitriolic attacks by elements of French rugby against European Cup chairman Jean-Pierre Lux for upholding the law and the principles of fair play in sport are astonishing and explain to an extent the resentment Agen have generated within certain sections of the public and media. To those, the defeat of Agen by Biarritz had all the ingredients of divine justice. Agen's abject capitulation against Ebbw Vale was explained at the time by the need to concentrate on the French Championship, with the underlying theme that ultimately the end justifies the means.

**PREVIOUS PAGE** Biarritz celebrate a try during their 30-10 home win over Leinster in Pool One of the 2001-02 Heineken Cup.

**BELOW** Nicolas Morlaes gets the ball away to his backs as Biarritz (in red and white) defeat Agen 25-22 in the final of the 2002 French Championship.

That is why Biarritz's championship final win, thanks to Laurent Mazas' extra-time dropped goal, was regarded by observers of the French scene not only as a success for your average French club but also as a defeat for the 'win at any cost' attitude that has beset French rugby since the days of shamateurism. But Biarritz's victory is probably more important than that, because the club's approach to success may offer French – and not only French – rugby a model for the future.

The funding of Biarritz is limited compared with the high-flyers of French rugby, Stade Français and Toulouse, although in Cap Gemini and its owner Serge Kampf the club has a benevolent sponsor and generous benefactor respectively. Biarritz, the city supporting the club, has less than 35,000 inhabitants, which forced the club, in order to expand their supporter base, to reinvent themselves as representatives of the Basque Country, calling themselves Biarritz-Olympique-Pays Basque.

Biarritz's success is based on a melange of hard-nosed business acumen, strong management, old-fashioned family philosophy and a very successful development programme. Their nursery is one of the most successful in France. The coaches are two mainstays of the Fouroux XV of the 1980s – No. 8 Laurent Rodriguez, the engine of the pack, and the 'Bayonne Express' Patrice Lagisquet, the lethal executioner on the left wing. The players thrive and develop in a club environment based on hard work, loyalty and respect, and if Biarritz are short of quality and expertise among their home-grown talent, they go and buy elsewhere.

However, Biarritz's signings are shrewd and comparatively inexpensive. The costs are controlled with an iron hand, whereas development is generously funded. Their 'acquisition' of Philippe Bernat-Salles, discarded for a variety of reasons by other clubs, was a major coup. It has paid off many times over, not only for the club but also for France, as the 'phantom striker' contributed to one of the biggest acts of destruction in international rugby – the French demolition of New Zealand in the semi-finals of RWC 1999. The Biarritz engine room contains two veterans, Olivier Roumat and

Philippe Versailles – thought by some clubs to be long past their sell-by date but who thrive in the special club environment. Thomas Lièvremont is another veteran whose career has been rejuvenated by the 'Biarritz diet' of hard work, care and sensible management.

Biarritz are also regarded as an eloquent and rational spokesman for the French professional clubs in their dealings with the FFR, and their success is proof that professionalism can be sensibly and successfully administered. The Biarritz success story, which commenced five years ago, is based on the strategic alliance between the club's most celebrated son, current chairman of the French Professional League Serge Blanco; Marcel Marie Martin, president of Biarritz Rugby Club and one of the world's most experienced administrators; the funds of Serge Kampf; and the talent and expertise of the duo Rodriguez & Lagisquet.

Martin, formerly a finance director of Mobil Oil Africa, is also a former general secretary and vice-president of the FFR and one-time IRB treasurer and RWC director whose expertise and know-how are still extensively used by RWC. He has set in place the financial framework that created the credibility platform for the club; he also helped secure the foreign recruits through his network of international contacts. Meanwhile, Blanco's charisma and astute man management acquired the support of Serge Kampf and Cap Gemini and the services of his former team-mates Lagisquet and Rodriguez as club coaches.

Nevertheless, Biarritz's rise to the fore of French rugby has not been as meteoric as all that. They have been working on it since 1996, which was when Marcel Martin stepped down from RWC to join the club. Three seasons ago they started to build the current team; two years ago they reached the knockout stages of the French Championship and did well in the European competitions. Last year Biarritz reached the semi-finals of the championship and had a very lucrative Heineken Cup campaign.

# Italy: Italian Rugby at the Crossroads

## by CHRIS THAU

'Irrespective of the rights and wrongs of the system, it is quite clear that many top Italian players are leaving the country for greener pastures, while the development path for talented youngsters is blocked by cheap foreign imports.'

The heap of files on the desk of the new Italian federation technical director, Bertrand Fourcade, is mounting as the former coach of Italy tries to sort out the development and elite selection issues confronting Italian rugby. 'Italian rugby is a pyramid upside down. Historically, grass-root development has not kept pace with the elite and we are in the odd situation of having more senior players than youth and juniors. The immediate objective is to increase the number of participants at grass roots,' he said recently.

At the same time he is trying to set in place the feeder system for Italy's Under 21 elite development, involving 120-150 players, which is essential for the prosperity of both the Under 21 and senior international programmes. Italy, fifth in the Under 21 Six Nations this year, have no Under 21 playing structure as such, and the technical and tactical shortcomings revealed by the Italian Under 21s in the World Cup in South Africa need urgent resolution if Italy are to develop a meaningful presence at top international level.

On the other hand, Italy have yet to win a senior Six Nations encounter since their so far solitary victory over Scotland in the opening match of the 1999-2000 competition. Italy have consistently failed to fulfil the early promise displayed during the reign of Georges Coste, sidelined by a players' revolt in 1999. Under Coste, Italy became a power to be reckoned with, with the 1994 tour of Australia as the highlight of their ascent to international status. His assistant, Massimo Mascioletti, replaced Coste just before RWC 1999, but the team collapsed to their worst display in RWC ever.

Mascioletti was unceremoniously dumped after the World Cup, and New Zealander Brad Johnstone, the former coach of Fiji, was hired to take Italy into the Six Nations Promised Land. He tried hard to instil the missing steel in the Italian approach, but was eventually forced to step down by the players, who requested the appointment of his assistant, John Kirwan, as national coach.

It might be too early to draw any conclusion, but the way two eminently capable coaches – known for their no-nonsense approach – have been undermined by senior players either unable or unprepared to take the extra step to close the gap with the rest of the world paints a not entirely edifying picture of the Italian camp. It may not take Kirwan, who played and coached in Italy, too much time before he identifies the source of the Italian malfunction, and because of his energetic attempt to bring in younger players, he already may have pinpointed the causes. But the odds are heavily stacked against him. Not only is the culture wrong but also the current structure is not designed to promote talent, hence the need for Fourcade's early intervention.

However, in his attempt to put Italian elite development on a more rational footing, Fourcade is facing an uphill battle, as revealed by the facts and figures of the final of the Italian Super 10, the grand name bestowed upon the first division of the Italian League, or *Scudetto*. Of the 41 players appearing in the Super 10 final for Arix Viadana and Ghial Amatori e Calvisano, 61 per cent were born outside Italy, with New Zealand leading the table with nine players, followed by Argentina with eight, Australia with four, South Africa with two and France and England with one each.

The majority of these players possess EC passports, which makes them eligible to ply their trade within the European Community. The small number of French and English players of quality in Italy suggests that Italian pay packages are inferior to those in France and England, which in turn determines the quality of the players employed in the Italian superleague.

Irrespective of the rights and wrongs of the system, it is quite clear that many top Italian players are leaving the country for greener pastures, while the development path for talented youngsters is blocked by cheap foreign imports. That is hardly the kind of stuff Fourcade is looking for to develop his teams of the future.

This situation is particularly destructive in Italy because of the small number of players, a fact Fourcade is painfully aware of. He plans to increase that number to about 40,000, while improving the quality of tuition, another major concern for the Italian technical director. Significantly, a similar flood of cheap foreign imports in France does not seem to affect French rugby too much, because there are ten times more players in France than in Italy.

*LEFT* Coach Georges Coste (right) made Italy a rugby power to be reckoned with. He stepped down in 1999 and was succeeded by his assistant, Massimo Mascioletti (left), who was replaced after Italy's poor showing in RWC 1999.

Fourcade may have to look into creating a regional competition for players eligible to play for Italy. A further option would be to enter those regional selections in the European Cup and Shield, but this may be legally difficult to achieve. Whatever he does, the Fourcade project is critical for the welfare of Italian rugby as FIR president Giancarlo Dondi acknowledged: 'The project Bertrand Fourcade has prepared is an investment in our future. We aim to increase the playing population to about 40.000 players. It is both quantity and quality we are looking for. The Six Nations Championship gave us an opportunity but this is not enough. We must deserve our place, by working harder to be competitive. I'm sure we will get there.'

# A Summary of the Season 2001-02

## by BILL MITCHELL

## INTERNATIONAL RUGBY

### AUSTRALIA TO CANADA & EUROPE
### OCTOBER & NOVEMBER 2001

| Opponents | Results |
|---|---|
| National Divisions XV | W 34-22 |
| SPAIN | W 92-10 |
| Oxford University | W 52-27 |
| ENGLAND | L 15-21 |
| FRANCE | L 13-14 |
| WALES | W 21-13 |
| Barbarians | W 49-35 |

Played 7 Won 5 Lost 2

### ARGENTINA TO WALES & SCOTLAND
### NOVEMBER 2001

| Opponents | Results |
|---|---|
| Wales 'A' | W 30-14 |
| WALES | W 30-16 |
| Scotland 'A' | L 35-40 |
| SCOTLAND | W 25-16 |

Played 4 Won 3 Lost 1

### ROMANIA TO ENGLAND
### NOVEMBER 2001

| Opponents | Results |
|---|---|
| England Students | W 21-11 |
| Combined Services | W 28-15 |
| ENGLAND | L 0-134 |

Played 3 Won 2 Lost 1

### SOUTH AFRICA TO EUROPE & UNITED STATES
### NOVEMBER 2001

| Opponents | Results |
|---|---|
| FRANCE | L 18-20 |
| ITALY | W 54-26 |
| ENGLAND | L 9-29 |
| UNITED STATES | W 43-20 |

Played 4 Won 2 Lost 2

### TONGA TO SCOTLAND & WALES
### NOVEMBER 2001

| Opponents | Results |
|---|---|
| Scotland 'A' | L 20-40 |
| SCOTLAND | L 20-43 |
| Wales 'A' | L 23-25 |
| WALES | L 7-51 |

Played 4 Lost 4

### URUGUAY TO WALES
### NOVEMBER 2001

| Opponents | Results |
|---|---|
| Newport | L 5-59 |
| Neath | L 3-29 |
| Wales 'A' | L 22-66 |

Played 3 Lost 3

### NEW ZEALAND TO EUROPE & SOUTH AMERICA
### NOVEMBER & DECEMBER 2001

| Opponents | Results |
|---|---|
| Ireland 'A' | W 43-30 |
| IRELAND | W 40-29 |
| Scotland 'A' | W 35-13 |
| SCOTLAND | W 37-6 |
| ARGENTINA | W 24-20 |

Played 5 Won 5

### SCOTLAND TO NORTH AMERICA
### JUNE 2002

| Opponents | Results |
|---|---|
| Canada East | W 38-8 |
| Rugby Canada | W 33-8 |
| Canada West | W 14-9 |
| CANADA | L 23-26 |
| United States 'A' | W 24-8 |
| UNITED STATES | W 65-23 |

Played 6 Won 5 Lost 1

## ITALY TO NEW ZEALAND
### JUNE 2002

| Opponents | Results |
|---|---|
| New Zealand Divisional XV | D 35-35 |
| NEW ZEALAND | L 10-64 |

Played 2 Drawn 1 Lost 1

## IRELAND TO NEW ZEALAND
### JUNE 2002

| Opponents | Results |
|---|---|
| New Zealand Divisional XV | W 56-3 |
| NEW ZEALAND | L 6-15 |
| NEW ZEALAND | L 8-40 |

Played 3 Won 1 Lost 2

## WALES TO SOUTH AFRICA
### JUNE 2002

| Opponents | Results |
|---|---|
| SOUTH AFRICA | L 19-34 |
| SOUTH AFRICA | L 8-19 |

Played 2 Lost 2

## ENGLAND TO ARGENTINA
### JUNE 2002

| Opponents | Results |
|---|---|
| Argentina 'A' | L 24-29 |
| ARGENTINA | W 26-18 |

Played 2 Won 1 Lost 1

## NEW ZEALAND MAORI TO AUSTRALIA
### JUNE 2002

| Opponents | Results |
|---|---|
| Queensland | L 25-28 |
| New South Wales | W 43-18 |
| AUSTRALIA | L 23-27 |

Played 3 Won 1 Lost 2

## FRANCE TO ARGENTINA & AUSTRALIA
### JUNE 2002

| Opponents | Results |
|---|---|
| ARGENTINA | L 27-28 |
| Australia 'A' | L 31-32 |
| AUSTRALIA | L 17-29 |
| Australia 'A' | L 34-37 |
| AUSTRALIA | L 25-31 |

Played 5 Lost 5

## LLOYDS TSB SIX NATIONS
### CHAMPIONSHIP 2001

*Delayed Results*

| Scotland | 32 | Ireland | 10 |
|---|---|---|---|
| Wales | 6 | Ireland | 36 |
| Ireland | 20 | England | 14 |

*Final Table*

| | P | W | D | L | F | A | Pts |
|---|---|---|---|---|---|---|---|
| England | 5 | 4 | 0 | 1 | 229 | 80 | 8 |
| Ireland | 5 | 4 | 0 | 1 | 129 | 89 | 8 |
| Scotland | 5 | 2 | 1 | 2 | 92 | 116 | 5 |
| Wales | 5 | 2 | 1 | 2 | 125 | 166 | 5 |
| France | 5 | 2 | 0 | 3 | 115 | 138 | 4 |
| Italy | 5 | 0 | 0 | 5 | 106 | 297 | 0 |

## LLOYDS TSB SIX NATIONS
### CHAMPIONSHIP 2002

*Results*

| France | 33 | Italy | 12 |
|---|---|---|---|
| Scotland | 3 | England | 29 |
| Ireland | 54 | Wales | 10 |
| England | 45 | Ireland | 11 |
| Italy | 12 | Scotland | 29 |
| Wales | 33 | France | 37 |
| France | 20 | England | 15 |
| Ireland | 43 | Scotland | 22 |
| Wales | 44 | Italy | 20 |
| England | 50 | Wales | 10 |
| Ireland | 32 | Italy | 17 |
| Scotland | 10 | France | 22 |
| France | 45 | Ireland | 5 |
| Wales | 22 | Scotland | 27 |
| Italy | 9 | England | 45 |

*Final Table*

| | P | W | D | L | F | A | Pts |
|---|---|---|---|---|---|---|---|
| France | 5 | 5 | 0 | 0 | 156 | 75 | 10 |
| England | 5 | 4 | 0 | 1 | 184 | 53 | 8 |
| Ireland | 5 | 3 | 0 | 2 | 145 | 138 | 6 |
| Scotland | 5 | 2 | 0 | 3 | 91 | 128 | 4 |
| Wales | 5 | 1 | 0 | 4 | 109 | 188 | 2 |
| Italy | 5 | 0 | 0 | 5 | 70 | 183 | 0 |

## OTHER INTERNATIONAL
### & REPRESENTATIVE MATCHES

*Results*

| Italy | 66 | Fiji | 10 |
|---|---|---|---|
| Ireland | 38 | Samoa | 8 |
| Fiji | 17 | French Barbarians | 15 |
| South Africa | 49 | Argentina | 29 |
| New Zealand | 68 | Fiji | 18 |
| South Africa | 60 | Samoa | 18 |

# Why use interaction?

Gather facts,
Facilitate decision making,
**Check understanding,** Vote,
Receive anonymous or Identified responses,
Provide quality meeting time, **Test Knowledge,**
**Reinforce training,**     Provide active role
Generate instant         for everyone,
reports & analysis,      **Find out what**
Gauge reactions,         **people think,**
**Empower**               Evaluate
**contributors,**         performance,
Offer an equal
opportunity for all,
Remove peer pressure,
**Speed up data gathering,**
Keep participants alert,
Measure changing perception,
Prove information
uptake,
**Reduce**
**administration**
**tasks,**
Create instant
rapport,

# iml

IML are market leaders supplying audience response voting systems to a global client base. We can add a dynamic element to your training, conference, product launches, exhibitions, sales presentations and market research.

Creating high quality multimedia presentations, we can enhance the benefit of our event through audience and presenter interaction. Not only will our system bring your meeting to life, but it will also ensure active audience participation.

Consequently, we can track an individual's progress. Perception and understanding for immediate and post event analysis. Our built-in microphone will also encourage active discussion and participation.

We are the "innovative group response" company.

For further information contact Matt Holmes on 01428 727476 or email mattholmes@iml.co.uk

IML Ltd 8 London Road Liphook Hampshire GU30 7AN United Kingdom
Tel: +44(0)1428 727476 Fax: +44(0)1428 727011 E-mail: marketing@iml.co.uk Website: www.iml.co.uk

## SIX NATIONS 'A' CHAMPIONSHIP 2002

*Results*

| | | | |
|---|---|---|---|
| Scotland | 6 | England | 6 |
| France | 28 | Italy | 13 |
| Ireland | 55 | Wales | 22 |
| England | 18 | Ireland | 25 |
| Italy | 26 | Scotland | 30 |
| Wales | 17 | France | 6 |
| France | 19 | England | 10 |
| Ireland | 60 | Scotland | 3 |
| Wales | 50 | Italy | 23 |
| England | 21 | Wales | 29 |
| Ireland | 59 | Italy | 5 |
| Scotland | 13 | France | 19 |
| France | 30 | Ireland | 20 |
| Wales | 30 | Scotland | 23 |
| Italy | 22 | England | 21 |

*Final Table*

| | P | W | D | L | F | A | Pts |
|---|---|---|---|---|---|---|---|
| Ireland | 5 | 4 | 0 | 1 | 219 | 78 | 8 |
| France | 5 | 4 | 0 | 1 | 102 | 73 | 8 |
| Wales | 5 | 4 | 0 | 1 | 148 | 128 | 8 |
| Scotland | 5 | 1 | 1 | 3 | 75 | 141 | 3 |
| Italy | 5 | 1 | 0 | 4 | 89 | 188 | 2 |
| England | 5 | 0 | 1 | 4 | 76 | 101 | 1 |

## SIX NATIONS UNDER 21 CHAMPIONSHIP 2002

*Results*

| | | | |
|---|---|---|---|
| Scotland | 16 | England | 31 |
| France | 62 | Italy | 3 |
| Ireland | 36 | Wales | 38 |
| England | 28 | Ireland | 23 |
| Italy | 6 | Scotland | 3 |
| Wales | 22 | France | 30 |
| France | 21 | England | 19 |
| Ireland | 25 | Scotland | 18 |
| Wales | 65 | Italy | 12 |
| England | 35 | Wales | 36 |
| Ireland | 60 | Italy | 14 |
| Scotland | 3 | France | 31 |
| France | 22 | Ireland | 21 |
| Wales | 64 | Scotland | 20 |
| Italy | 15 | England | 50 |

*Final Table*

| | P | W | D | L | F | A | Pts |
|---|---|---|---|---|---|---|---|
| France | 5 | 5 | 0 | 0 | 166 | 68 | 10 |
| Wales | 5 | 4 | 0 | 1 | 225 | 133 | 8 |
| Ireland | 5 | 3 | 0 | 2 | 171 | 120 | 6 |
| England | 5 | 2 | 0 | 3 | 163 | 117 | 4 |
| Italy | 5 | 1 | 0 | 4 | 50 | 240 | 2 |
| Scotland | 5 | 0 | 0 | 5 | 60 | 157 | 0 |

## UNDER 21 WORLD CUP 2002

(Held in Johannesburg, South Africa)

*Seventh-place Play-off:*

| | | | |
|---|---|---|---|
| England | 74 | Argentina | 14 |

*Fifth-place Play-off*

| | | | |
|---|---|---|---|
| France | 40 | Ireland | 29 |

*Semi-finals*

| | | | |
|---|---|---|---|
| Australia | 43 | Wales | 7 |
| South Africa | 19 | New Zealand | 18 |

*Third-place Play-off*

| | | | |
|---|---|---|---|
| New Zealand | 59 | Wales | 7 |

*Final*

| | | | |
|---|---|---|---|
| South Africa | 24 | Australia | 21 |

## UNDER 19 WORLD CHAMPIONSHIP 2002

(Held in Treviso, Italy)

*Seventh-place Play-off*

| | | | |
|---|---|---|---|
| Wales | 19 | Italy | 15 |

*Fifth-place Play-off*

| | | | |
|---|---|---|---|
| Scotland | 17 | England | 10 |

*Semi-finals*

| | | | |
|---|---|---|---|
| France | 20 | Argentina | 6 |
| New Zealand | 41 | South Africa | 9 |

*Third-place Play-off*

| | | | |
|---|---|---|---|
| South Africa | 5 | Argentina | 19 |

*Final*

| | | | |
|---|---|---|---|
| New Zealand | 71 | France | 18 |

## HOME NATIONS SCHOOLS TOURNAMENT 2002

(Held at Easter in Otley, West Yorkshire)

*Results*

| | | | |
|---|---|---|---|
| England | 17 | Scotland | 10 |
| Wales | 20 | Ireland | 5 |
| Wales | 16 | Scotland | 16 |
| England | 18 | Ireland | 20 |
| England | 19 | Wales | 23 |
| Scotland | 36 | Ireland | 11 |

*Final Table*

| | P | W | D | L | F | A | Pts |
|---|---|---|---|---|---|---|---|
| Wales | 3 | 2 | 1 | 0 | 59 | 40 | 5 |
| Scotland | 3 | 1 | 1 | 1 | 62 | 44 | 3 |
| England | 3 | 1 | 0 | 2 | 54 | 53 | 2 |
| Ireland | 3 | 1 | 0 | 2 | 36 | 74 | 2 |

## OTHER SCHOOLS AND AGE GROUPS MATCHES

*Results*

| | | | |
|---|---|---|---|
| England U19 | 12 | Wales U19 | 0 |
| England U19 | 15 | Ireland U19 | 0 |
| Wales U19 | 19 | France U19 | 17 |
| Italy U19 | 7 | Scotland U19 | 61 |

## INTERNATIONAL UNIVERSITIES TROPHY 2001-02

*Final*

| | | | |
|---|---|---|---|
| U of Wales (Swansea) | 7 | University of Pau | 37 |

## OTHER STUDENT AND UNIVERSITY INTERNATIONALS 2001-02

*Results*

| | | | |
|---|---|---|---|
| Scotland Students | 14 | England Students | 19 |
| Scotland Universities | 8 | England Universities | 38 |
| England Students | 17 | Ireland Students | 18 |
| Ireland Students | 17 | Scotland Students | 12 |
| Scotland Students | 8 | France Students | 25 |
| Wales Students | 29 | Scotland Students | 32 |

## HONG KONG SEVENS 2002

*Cup Final*

| | | | |
|---|---|---|---|
| England | 33 | Fiji | 20 |

*Plate Final*

| | | | |
|---|---|---|---|
| South Africa | 48 | Scotland | 7 |

*Bowl Final*

| | | | |
|---|---|---|---|
| Morocco | 15 | Chinese Taipei | 12 |

## IRB SEVENS FINALS 2001-02

*Durban (South Africa)*

| | | | |
|---|---|---|---|
| New Zealand | 19 | Samoa | 17 |

*Santiago (Chile)*

| | | | |
|---|---|---|---|
| New Zealand | 21 | Argentina | 7 |

*Mar del Plata (Argentina)*

| | | | |
|---|---|---|---|
| Fiji | 24 | South Africa | 7 |

*Brisbane (Australia)*

| | | | |
|---|---|---|---|
| Australia | 28 | New Zealand | 0 |

*Wellington (New Zealand)*

| | | | |
|---|---|---|---|
| South Africa | 17 | Samoa | 14 |

*Beijing (China)*

| | | | |
|---|---|---|---|
| New Zealand | 41 | South Africa | 14 |

*Singapore*

| | | | |
|---|---|---|---|
| New Zealand | 21 | Argentina | 17 |

*Kuala Lumpur (Malaysia)*

| | | | |
|---|---|---|---|
| New Zealand | 29 | South Africa | 5 |

*Emirates London Sevens (Twickenham)*

| | | | |
|---|---|---|---|
| New Zealand | 54 | South Africa | 14 |

*Emirates Cardiff Sevens (Millennium Stadium)*

| | | | |
|---|---|---|---|
| New Zealand | 24 | England | 12 |

*New Zealand win the IRB Sevens Series*

## COMMONWEALTH GAMES 2002 SEVENS

(Held in Manchester)

*Semi-finals*

| | | | |
|---|---|---|---|
| New Zealand | 31 | Samoa | 7 |
| Fiji | 17 | South Africa | 7 |

*Bronze Medal Play-off*

| | | | |
|---|---|---|---|
| South Africa | 19 | Samoa | 12 |

*Final*

| | | | |
|---|---|---|---|
| New Zealand | 33 | Fiji | 15 |

*Plate Final (no medals)*

| | | | |
|---|---|---|---|
| England | 36 | Australia | 12 |

*Bowl Final (no medals)*

| | | | |
|---|---|---|---|
| Scotland | 40 | Tonga | 26 |

## OTHER INTERNATIONAL SEVENS WINNERS

*Safari Sevens (Nairobi, Kenya)*
British Army

## TRI-NATIONS 2002

*Results*

| | | | |
|---|---|---|---|
| New Zealand | 12 | Australia | 6 |
| New Zealand | 41 | South Africa | 20 |
| Australia | 38 | South Africa | 27 |
| Australia | 16 | New Zealand | 14 |
| South Africa | 23 | New Zealand | 30 |
| South Africa | 33 | Australia | 31 |

## WOMEN'S SIX NATIONS CHAMPIONSHIP 2002

*Results*

| | | | |
|---|---|---|---|
| France | 20 | Spain | 0 |
| Scotland | 8 | England | 35 |
| Ireland | 9 | Wales | 13 |
| Wales | 0 | France | 24 |
| England | 79 | Ireland | 0 |
| Spain | 14 | Scotland | 17 |
| France | 22 | England | 17 |
| Ireland | 0 | Scotland | 13 |
| Wales | 0 | Spain | 16 |
| Scotland | 12 | France | 22 |
| England | 40 | Wales | 0 |
| Ireland | 6 | Wales | 8 |
| France | 46 | Ireland | 0 |
| Spain | 14 | England | 53 |
| Wales | 3 | Scotland | 31 |

*Final Table*

| | P | W | D | L | F | A | Pts |
|---|---|---|---|---|---|---|---|
| France | 5 | 5 | 0 | 0 | 134 | 29 | 10 |
| England | 5 | 4 | 0 | 1 | 224 | 44 | 8 |
| Scotland | 5 | 3 | 0 | 2 | 81 | 74 | 6 |
| Spain | 5 | 2 | 0 | 3 | 56 | 100 | 4 |
| Wales | 5 | 1 | 0 | 4 | 16 | 120 | 2 |
| Ireland | 5 | 0 | 0 | 5 | 15 | 159 | 0 |

## WOMEN'S WORLD CUP 2002

(Held in Spain)

*Quarter-finals*

| | | | |
|---|---|---|---|
| Spain | 5 | England | 11 |
| Canada | 11 | Scotland | 0 |
| France | 21 | United States | 9 |
| New Zealand | 36 | Australia | 3 |

*Semi-finals*

| | | | |
|---|---|---|---|
| New Zealand | 30 | France | 0 |
| England | 53 | Canada | 10 |

*Final*

| | | | |
|---|---|---|---|
| New Zealand | 19 | England | 9 |

# CLUB, COUNTY AND DIVISIONAL RUGBY

## ENGLAND

### Powergen Cup
*Quarter-finals*

| | | | |
|---|---|---|---|
| Harlequins | 22 | Leicester | 20 |
| Saracens | 28 | Northampton | 30 |
| Leeds | 24 | Newcastle | 41 |
| London Irish | 25 | Gloucester | 10 |

*Semi-finals*

| | | | |
|---|---|---|---|
| Harlequins | 27 | London Irish | 32 |
| Northampton | 38 | Newcastle | 7 |

*Final*

| | | | |
|---|---|---|---|
| London Irish | 38 | Northampton | 7 |

### Zurich Premiership

| | P | W | D | L | F | A | PD | Pts |
|---|---|---|---|---|---|---|---|---|
| Leicester | 22 | 18 | 0 | 4 | 658 | 349 | 309 | 83 |
| Sale | 22 | 14 | 1 | 7 | 589 | 517 | 72 | 69 |
| Gloucester | 22 | 14 | 0 | 8 | 692 | 485 | 207 | 68 |
| London Irish | 22 | 11 | 3 | 8 | 574 | 465 | 109 | 57 |
| Northampton | 22 | 12 | 1 | 9 | 506 | 426 | 80 | 56 |
| Newcastle | 22 | 12 | 1 | 9 | 490 | 458 | 32 | 56 |
| Wasps | 22 | 12 | 0 | 10 | 519 | 507 | 12 | 54 |
| Bristol | 22 | 9 | 1 | 12 | 591 | 632 | -41 | 50 |
| Harlequins | 22 | 5 | 3 | 14 | 434 | 507 | -73 | 35 |
| Saracens | 22 | 7 | 0 | 15 | 425 | 671 | -246 | 34 |
| Bath | 22 | 7 | 0 | 15 | 311 | 524 | -213 | 33 |
| Leeds | 22 | 6 | 0 | 16 | 406 | 654 | -248 | 28 |

### Zurich Premiership Play-offs
*Quarter-finals*

| | | | |
|---|---|---|---|
| Gloucester | 60 | Newcastle | 9 |
| Leicester | 13 | Bristol | 27 |
| London Irish | 14 | Northampton | 38 |
| Sale | 43 | Wasps | 27 |

*Semi-finals*

| | | | |
|---|---|---|---|
| Bristol | 32 | Northampton | 24 |
| Sale | 11 | Gloucester | 33 |

*Final*

| | | | |
|---|---|---|---|
| Gloucester | 28 | Bristol | 23 |

### National Leagues
1st Division Champions: Rotherham
Runners-up: Worcester
2nd Division Champions: Orrell
Runners-up: Plymouth Albion
3rd Division North Champions: Doncaster
Runners-up: Dudley Kingswinford
3rd Division South Champions: Penzance & Newlyn
Runners-up: Launceston

### Powergen Intermediate Cup Final

| | | | |
|---|---|---|---|
| Halifax | 43 | G'port & Fareham | 19 |

### Powergen Junior Cup Final:

| | | | |
|---|---|---|---|
| Heath | 16 | Bromley | 10 |

### Powergen Challenge Shield Final

| | | | |
|---|---|---|---|
| Rotherham | 35 | Exeter | 26 |

### U21 Championship
Winners: Bristol
Runners-up: Wasps

### U21 Championship Final

| | | | |
|---|---|---|---|
| Wasps | 38 | Bristol | 7 |

### Tetley's Bitter U20 County Championship Final

| | | | |
|---|---|---|---|
| Hampshire | 27 | Cornwall | 14 |

### Middlesex Charity Sevens Cup Final

| | | | |
|---|---|---|---|
| Bradford Bulls | 42 | Wasps | 14 |

### Tetley's National Counties Seven-a-Sides Final

| | | | |
|---|---|---|---|
| Yorkshire | 42 | Cornwall | 26 |

### Women's County Sevens Final

| | | | |
|---|---|---|---|
| Oxfordshire | 29 | Lancashire | 12 |

### University Match

| | | | |
|---|---|---|---|
| Oxford U | 9 | Cambridge U | 6 |

### University Second Teams Match

| | | | |
|---|---|---|---|
| OU Greyhounds | 20 | CU LX Club | 30 |

### University U21 Match

| | | | |
|---|---|---|---|
| Oxford U | 23 | Cambridge U | 17 |

### Other University U21 Match

| | | | |
|---|---|---|---|
| Cambridge U21 'A' | 10 | OU Whippets | 13 |

### Colleges Match

| | | | |
|---|---|---|---|
| Cambridge U | 7 | Oxford U | 0 |

### Women's University Match

| | | | |
|---|---|---|---|
| Oxford U | 5 | Cambridge U | 29 |

### Halifax British Universities Sports Association
*Men's Final*

| | | | |
|---|---|---|---|
| Brunel West London | 25 | St Mary's UC | 23 |

*Women's Final*

| | | | |
|---|---|---|---|
| Cardiff Institute | 23 | Loughborough | 7 |

### Services/Universities Tournament

| | P | W | D | L | F | A | Pts |
|---|---|---|---|---|---|---|---|
| Oxford Univ | 4 | 4 | 0 | 0 | 108 | 50 | 8 |
| Cambridge Univ | 4 | 3 | 0 | 1 | 104 | 40 | 6 |
| Army | 4 | 2 | 0 | 2 | 119 | 81 | 4 |
| Royal Navy | 4 | 1 | 0 | 3 | 60 | 97 | 2 |
| Royal Air Force | 4 | 0 | 0 | 4 | 52 | 175 | 0 |

**Hospitals Cup Winners:** Imperial Medicals
**Inter-Services Champions:** Army
### The Army Rosslyn Park Schools Sevens
Festival Winners: Wellington College
Junior Winners: Brynteg School
Preparatory Schools Winners: The Downs
Open Cup Winners: Millfield School
*NB: The Girls and Colts events were cancelled owing to waterlogged pitches*
### Daily Mail Schools Day (at Twickenham)
U18 Cup Winners: Oakham School
U18 Vase Winners: Solihull School
U15 Cup Winners: St Peter's School, York

### Women's National Cup Final

| | | | |
|---|---|---|---|
| Clifton | 54 | Nottingham MC | 7 |

### Women's National Sevens Final

| | | | |
|---|---|---|---|
| Wasps | 40 | Saracens | 5 |

**Sporting Index**

World Leaders in Sports Spread Betting

# OPEN AN ACCOUNT WITH THE MARKET LEADERS

## NO OTHER SPREAD BETTING COMPANY OFFERS YOU ALL THIS:

**FREE £250 BET AFTER JUST 5 BETS!**

**Live, Interactive On-Line Betting**
24hrs a day, 7 days a week

**FREEPHONE Betting and Customer Service Lines**

**The widest range of live 'IN-RUNNING' sports on which to bet**

**The choice of two accounts:**

 **Classic** ACCOUNT — *Giving you the freedom to bet with the stakes to suit you.*

**Shield** ACCOUNT — *The lowest deposit terms and stakes in the industry.*

## To open an account call 08000 96 96 45 NOW
## or register at www.SportingIndex.com

## SCOTLAND

### Inter-District Championship

|           | P | W | D | L | F   | A   | BP | Pts |
|-----------|---|---|---|---|-----|-----|----|-----|
| Borders   | 4 | 4 | 0 | 0 | 142 | 57  | 2  | 18  |
| Glasgow   | 4 | 3 | 0 | 1 | 100 | 70  | 2  | 14  |
| Scot Exiles | 4 | 2 | 0 | 2 | 91 | 74  | 1  | 9   |
| Caledonia | 4 | 1 | 0 | 3 | 77  | 99  | 2  | 6   |
| Edinburgh | 4 | 0 | 0 | 4 | 66  | 176 | 1  | 1   |

### BT Cellnet Cup Final
Hawick      20   Glasgow Hawks   17
(after extra-time)

### BT Cellnet Shield Final
Kirkcaldy     41   Stewartry     12

### BT Cellnet Bowl Final
Ellon      18   Hawick Harlequins   6

### Scottish Borders Sevens Winners
Kelso: Kelso
Selkirk: Royal Scots
Melrose: Boroughmuir
Peebles: Peebles
Hawick: Jed-Forest
Langholm: Melrose
Earlston: Melrose
Jed-Forest: Watsonians
Gala: Royal Scots
Berwick: Melrose
Kings of Sevens: Melrose

### BT Scotland Premiership
Division One

|              | P  | W  | D | L  | F   | A   | BP | Pts |
|--------------|----|----|---|----|-----|-----|----|-----|
| Hawick       | 18 | 15 | 1 | 2  | 505 | 284 | 10 | 72  |
| Boroughmuir  | 18 | 15 | 0 | 3  | 488 | 291 | 11 | 71  |
| Heriot's FP  | 18 | 10 | 0 | 8  | 501 | 330 | 10 | 50  |
| Aberdeen GS FP | 18 | 9 | 0 | 9 | 369 | 393 | 8  | 44  |
| Glasgow Hawks | 18 | 8 | 0 | 10 | 379 | 371 | 9  | 41  |
| Melrose      | 18 | 9  | 0 | 9  | 325 | 439 | 5  | 41  |
| Stirling Cty | 18 | 8  | 0 | 10 | 345 | 385 | 7  | 39  |
| Currie       | 18 | 7  | 0 | 11 | 393 | 459 | 9  | 37  |
| Gala         | 18 | 6  | 2 | 10 | 314 | 433 | 4  | 32  |
| Kirkcaldy    | 18 | 1  | 1 | 16 | 234 | 468 | 3  | 9   |

*Champions: Hawick*
*Relegated: Gala, Kirkcaldy*

Division Two

|                | P  | W  | D | L  | F   | A   | BP | Pts |
|----------------|----|----|---|----|-----|-----|----|-----|
| Peebles        | 18 | 16 | 1 | 1  | 393 | 218 | 6  | 72  |
| Jed-Forest     | 18 | 14 | 0 | 4  | 455 | 251 | 9  | 65  |
| Watsonians     | 18 | 11 | 0 | 7  | 410 | 322 | 8  | 52  |
| Ayr            | 18 | 10 | 0 | 8  | 437 | 295 | 9  | 49  |
| Kelso          | 18 | 6  | 1 | 11 | 356 | 358 | 9  | 35  |
| Selkirk        | 18 | 7  | 0 | 11 | 287 | 425 | 7  | 35  |
| Murrayfield Wdrs | 18 | 7 | 0 | 11 | 316 | 465 | 6 | 34  |
| Grangemouth    | 18 | 5  | 0 | 13 | 339 | 393 | 11 | 31  |
| East Kilbride  | 18 | 6  | 0 | 12 | 270 | 394 | 6  | 30  |
| W of Scotland  | 18 | 7  | 0 | 11 | 279 | 422 | 1  | 29  |

*Promoted: Peebles (Champions), Jed-Forest*
*Relegated: West of Scotland, East Kilbride*

## WALES

### Principality Cup
*Quarter-finals*

| Cardiff    | 20 | Newport   | 14 |
|------------|----|-----------|----|
| Llanelli   | 46 | Bridgend  | 21 |
| Pontypool  | 22 | Ebbw Vale | 27 |
| Pontypridd | 46 | Caerphilly | 31 |

*Semi-finals*

| Llanelli   | 34 | Ebbw Vale | 17 |
|------------|----|-----------|----|
| Pontypridd | 31 | Cardiff   | 25 |

*Final*

| Pontypridd | 20 | Llanelli | 17 |
|------------|----|----------|----|

### Welsh/Scottish League Premier Division

|            | P  | W  | D | L  | F   | A   | T  | Pts |
|------------|----|----|---|----|-----|-----|----|-----|
| Llanelli   | 20 | 15 | 0 | 5  | 582 | 402 | 60 | 45  |
| Newport    | 20 | 14 | 1 | 5  | 576 | 415 | 64 | 43  |
| Neath      | 20 | 14 | 0 | 6  | 616 | 366 | 64 | 42  |
| Cardiff    | 20 | 13 | 1 | 6  | 498 | 404 | 56 | 40  |
| Swansea    | 20 | 11 | 0 | 9  | 451 | 404 | 42 | 33  |
| Edinburgh  | 20 | 10 | 2 | 8  | 498 | 512 | 56 | 32  |
| Pontypridd | 20 | 9  | 0 | 11 | 441 | 440 | 41 | 27  |
| Glasgow    | 20 | 8  | 1 | 11 | 475 | 527 | 50 | 25  |
| Bridgend   | 20 | 7  | 1 | 12 | 498 | 545 | 46 | 22  |
| Ebbw Vale  | 20 | 5  | 0 | 15 | 407 | 609 | 36 | 15  |
| Caerphilly | 20 | 1  | 0 | 19 | 379 | 798 | 40 | 3   |

*Champions: Llanelli*
*Relegation play-off won by Caerphilly*
*In 2002-03 the league will continue without Glasgow and Edinburgh and will comprise ten Welsh clubs*

### Welsh National Leagues
Division One

|              | P  | W  | D | L  | F    | A    | Pts |
|--------------|----|----|---|----|------|------|-----|
| Aberavon     | 32 | 27 | 0 | 5  | 1124 | 469  | 81  |
| Pontypool    | 32 | 27 | 0 | 5  | 1138 | 532  | 81  |
| Carmarthen Qns | 32 | 23 | 1 | 8 | 871 | 475  | 70  |
| Newbridge    | 32 | 22 | 0 | 10 | 871  | 471  | 66  |
| Tondu        | 32 | 20 | 1 | 11 | 739  | 634  | 61  |
| Llandovery   | 32 | 20 | 0 | 12 | 909  | 696  | 60  |
| Blackwood    | 32 | 19 | 2 | 11 | 700  | 631  | 59  |
| Bedwas       | 32 | 18 | 3 | 11 | 679  | 629  | 57  |
| Rumney       | 32 | 13 | 1 | 18 | 662  | 680  | 40  |
| Whitland     | 32 | 12 | 2 | 18 | 478  | 678  | 38  |
| Cross Keys   | 32 | 12 | 0 | 20 | 670  | 789  | 36  |
| Treorchy     | 32 | 11 | 2 | 19 | 582  | 741  | 35  |
| Bonymaen     | 32 | 10 | 0 | 22 | 611  | 848  | 30  |
| Llanharan    | 32 | 10 | 0 | 22 | 529  | 1019 | 30  |
| Glam'n Wdrs  | 32 | 9  | 1 | 22 | 650  | 936  | 28  |
| Dunvant      | 32 | 7  | 1 | 24 | 639  | 1007 | 22  |
| Merthyr      | 32 | 5  | 0 | 27 | 447  | 1063 | 15  |

*Champions: Aberavon (not promoted)*
*Relegated: Dunvant, Merthyr*

2nd Division Champions: Narberth
Runners-up: Beddau
3rd Division East Champions: Llantwit Fardre
Runners-up: Hirwaun
3rd Division West Champions: Cwmavon
Runners-up: British Steel (Port Talbot)

## IRELAND

### Celtic League
*Semi-finals*

| | | | |
|---|---|---|---|
| Leinster | 35 | Glasgow | 13 |
| Munster | 15 | Ulster | 9 |

*Final*

| | | | |
|---|---|---|---|
| Leinster | 24 | Munster | 20 |

### Inter-Provincial Championship

| | P | W | D | L | F | A | BP | Pts |
|---|---|---|---|---|---|---|---|---|
| Leinster | 3 | 2 | 1 | 0 | 86 | 35 | 2 | 12 |
| Ulster | 3 | 2 | 0 | 1 | 50 | 66 | 0 | 8 |
| Munster | 3 | 1 | 1 | 1 | 64 | 47 | 1 | 7 |
| Connacht | 3 | 0 | 0 | 3 | 56 | 107 | 1 | 1 |

### AIB League
Division One

| | P | W | D | L | F | A | BP | Pts |
|---|---|---|---|---|---|---|---|---|
| Cork Constitution | 15 | 11 | 2 | 2 | 314 | 191 | 4 | 52 |
| Shannon | 15 | 11 | 1 | 3 | 359 | 209 | 5 | 51 |
| Clontarf | 15 | 10 | 1 | 4 | 354 | 225 | 5 | 47 |
| Garryowen | 15 | 9 | 2 | 4 | 357 | 259 | 5 | 45 |
| St Mary's Coll | 15 | 9 | 1 | 5 | 298 | 285 | 5 | 43 |
| UC Dublin | 15 | 8 | 1 | 6 | 358 | 379 | 5 | 39 |
| Galwegians | 15 | 8 | 0 | 7 | 322 | 302 | 6 | 38 |
| Terenure College | 15 | 8 | 0 | 7 | 294 | 294 | 4 | 36 |
| Blackrock College | 15 | 6 | 1 | 8 | 357 | 339 | 8 | 34 |
| Dungannon | 15 | 6 | 1 | 8 | 283 | 305 | 6 | 32 |
| Ballymena | 15 | 6 | 0 | 9 | 259 | 281 | 6 | 30 |
| Buccaneers | 15 | 5 | 2 | 8 | 297 | 288 | 5 | 29 |
| Lansdowne | 15 | 5 | 1 | 9 | 272 | 308 | 5 | 27 |
| County Carlow | 15 | 5 | 1 | 9 | 259 | 383 | 4 | 26 |
| De la Salle-P'ton | 15 | 4 | 0 | 11 | 251 | 407 | 5 | 21 |
| Young Munster | 15 | 2 | 0 | 13 | 209 | 384 | 4 | 12 |

*Final:*

| | | | |
|---|---|---|---|
| Shannon | 21 | Cork Constitution | 17 |

*Relegated: De la Salle-Palmerston, Young Munster*

Division Two

| | P | W | D | L | F | A | BP | Pts |
|---|---|---|---|---|---|---|---|---|
| Belfast H'quins | 15 | 14 | 0 | 1 | 549 | 249 | 12 | 68 |
| UL Bohemians | 15 | 11 | 1 | 3 | 301 | 218 | 4 | 50 |
| Barnhall | 15 | 11 | 1 | 3 | 283 | 220 | 4 | 50 |
| Old Crescent | 15 | 11 | 0 | 4 | 292 | 208 | 4 | 48 |
| Old Belvedere | 15 | 7 | 2 | 6 | 373 | 276 | 9 | 41 |
| Malone | 15 | 8 | 1 | 6 | 294 | 271 | 4 | 38 |
| Bective Rangers | 15 | 7 | 1 | 7 | 323 | 317 | 6 | 36 |
| *Ballynahinch | 15 | 9 | 0 | 6 | 247 | 274 | 4 | 36 |
| Midleton | 15 | 7 | 1 | 7 | 209 | 222 | 4 | 34 |
| Thomond | 15 | 6 | 1 | 8 | 259 | 244 | 7 | 33 |
| Portadown | 15 | 5 | 0 | 10 | 244 | 289 | 7 | 31 |
| Univ College Cork | 15 | 5 | 1 | 9 | 255 | 366 | 4 | 26 |
| Sunday's Well | 15 | 4 | 1 | 10 | 241 | 323 | 6 | 24 |
| Dolphin | 15 | 5 | 0 | 10 | 242 | 338 | 6 | 22 |
| Wanderers | 15 | 2 | 0 | 13 | 180 | 333 | 7 | 15 |
| +City of Derry | 15 | 3 | 0 | 12 | 196 | 340 | 6 | 10 |

*\* Four points deducted; + Eight points deducted*
*Promoted: Belfast Harlequins, UL Bohemians*
*Relegated: Wanderers, City of Derry*

## FRANCE

### French Championship
Pool A

| | P | W | D | L | F | A | Pts |
|---|---|---|---|---|---|---|---|
| Biarritz | 6 | 4 | 1 | 1 | 153 | 122 | 15 |
| Agen | 6 | 3 | 1 | 2 | 163 | 116 | 13 |
| Bourgoin | 6 | 2 | 1 | 3 | 127 | 179 | 11 |
| Stade Français | 6 | 0 | 3 | 3 | 133 | 159 | 9 |

Pool B

| | P | W | D | L | F | A | Pts |
|---|---|---|---|---|---|---|---|
| Toulouse | 6 | 5 | 0 | 1 | 198 | 120 | 16 |
| Montferrand | 6 | 3 | 0 | 3 | 146 | 161 | 12 |
| Perpignan | 6 | 2 | 0 | 4 | 127 | 154 | 10 |
| Béziers | 6 | 2 | 0 | 4 | 137 | 173 | 10 |

*Semi-finals*

| | | | |
|---|---|---|---|
| Agen | 21 | Toulouse | 12 |
| Biarritz | 31 | Montferrand | 12 |

*Final*

| | | | |
|---|---|---|---|
| Biarritz | 25 | Agen | 22 |
| (after extra time) | | | |

## ITALY

### Italian Championship
*Final*

| | | | |
|---|---|---|---|
| Arix Viadana | 19 | GA & Calvisano | 12 |

## NEW ZEALAND

### National Provincial Championship

*Semi-finals*

| | | | |
|---|---|---|---|
| Canterbury | 53 | Auckland | 22 |
| Otago | 37 | North Harbour | 10 |

*Final*

| | | | |
|---|---|---|---|
| Canterbury | 30 | Otago | 19 |

**Ranfurly Shield holders:** Canterbury

## AUSTRALIA

**Champions 2001:** ACT Brumbies

## SOUTH AFRICA

**Currie Cup 2001**

*Final*

| | | | |
|---|---|---|---|
| Western Stormers | 29 | Natal Coastal Sharks | 24 |

## BARBARIANS

| Opponents | Results |
|---|---|
| Combined Services | W 50-14 |
| AUSTRALIA | L 35-49 |
| East Midlands | W 66-35 |
| ENGLAND | L 29-53 |
| WALES | W 40-25 |
| SCOTLAND | W 47-27 |

Played 6 Won 4 Lost 2

## SUPER 12 TOURNAMENT 2002

*Final table*

|  | P | W | L | F | A | BP | Pts |
|---|---|---|---|---|---|---|---|
| Crusaders | 11 | 11 | 0 | 469 | 264 | 7 | 51 |
| Waratahs | 11 | 8 | 3 | 337 | 284 | 7 | 39 |
| Brumbies | 11 | 7 | 4 | 374 | 230 | 10 | 38 |
| Highlanders | 11 | 8 | 3 | 329 | 207 | 6 | 38 |
| Reds | 11 | 7 | 4 | 336 | 287 | 6 | 34 |
| Blues | 11 | 6 | 5 | 318 | 249 | 5 | 29 |
| Stormers | 11 | 5 | 6 | 310 | 314 | 7 | 27 |
| Chiefs | 11 | 4 | 7 | 323 | 341 | 8 | 24 |
| Hurricanes | 11 | 5 | 6 | 232 | 317 | 3 | 23 |
| Sharks | 11 | 4 | 7 | 221 | 309 | 4 | 20 |
| Cats | 11 | 1 | 10 | 228 | 407 | 2 | 6 |
| Bulls | 11 | 0 | 11 | 232 | 500 | 4 | 4 |

*Semi-finals*

| Crusaders | 34 | Highlanders | 23 |
|---|---|---|---|
| (Christchurch) | | | |
| Waratahs | 10 | Brumbies | 51 |
| (Sydney) | | | |

*Final*

| Crusaders | 34 | Brumbies | 13 |
|---|---|---|---|
| (Christchurch) | | | |

## EUROPEAN CUP

*Quarter-finals*

| Bath | 10 | Llanelli | 24 |
|---|---|---|---|
| Castres | 22 | Montferrand | 21 |
| Leicester | 29 | Leinster | 18 |
| Stade Français | 14 | Munster | 16 |

*Semi-finals*

| Castres | 17 | Munster | 25 |
|---|---|---|---|
| Leicester | 13 | Llanelli | 12 |

*Final*

| Leicester | 15 | Munster | 9 |
|---|---|---|---|

## EUROPEAN SHIELD

*Quarter-finals*

| Gloucester | 46 | Ebbw Vale | 11 |
|---|---|---|---|
| Pau | 9 | London Irish | 38 |
| Sale | 25 | Bristol | 20 |
| Saracens | 15 | Pontypridd | 17 |

*Semi-finals*

| Gloucester | 27 | Sale | 28 |
|---|---|---|---|
| London Irish | 27 | Pontypridd | 33 |

*Final*

| Sale | 25 | Pontypridd | 22 |
|---|---|---|---|

**BEHIND SCOTTISH RUGBY.**

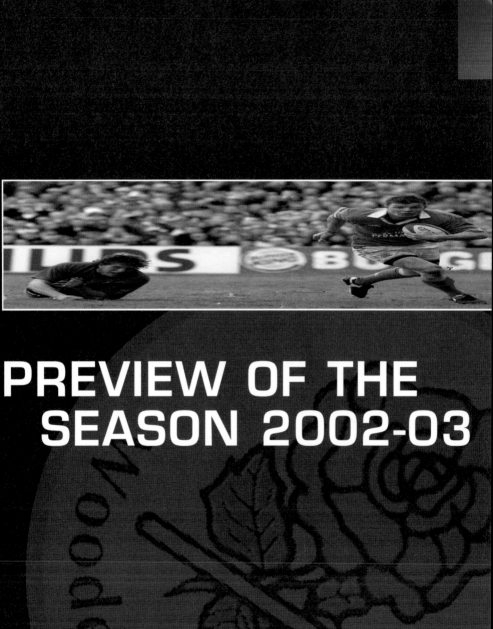

# PREVIEW OF THE
# SEASON 2002-03

# Key Players 2002-03

## by IAN ROBERTSON

### ENGLAND

| JONNY WILKINSON |
| --- |

No England international rugby player in living memory has achieved so much in such a short time as Jonny Wilkinson. By the end of the 2002 Six Nations, when he was only 22 years of age, he had already become the first England player to score over 500 points in Test rugby and he had also won 35 caps. With a possible 20 Tests for England between November 2002 and November 2003, he could be one of the top half-dozen points scorers in the history of Test rugby by the end of the World Cup, and he would still be in his early twenties. He is not just arguably the best goal-kicker in world rugby, he is also an outstanding fly half. He is probably the best and most aggressive defensive fly half in the game, and his tackling is so dynamic he performs as if he is an extra flanker. His handling and distribution are second to none, and in the past 12 months he has also become much more adventurous in attack, fully capable of making breaks and creating space for his threequarters. He is equally important to the England team as a great defensive player, a brilliant goal-kicker, an attacking fly half and a natural leader.

| BEN KAY |
| --- |

It must have been a great advantage for Ben Kay to learn the tricks of the trade playing alongside the Leicester, England and Lions lock, Martin Johnson. He arrived at Leicester with a pretty good pedigree. He gained his first representative honours when he played for England in the Students World Cup in South Africa in 1996 and went on to play for England 'A' before winning his first full cap in June 2001. This promotion came on the back of two outstanding seasons with Leicester, in which he played a major role in helping to make Leicester's pack the best in the Zurich Premiership. He is now an invaluable member of the Tigers team and he was a real force when they won the Heineken Cup for the first time last year. He settled in to the greater speed and intensity of international rugby with remarkable ease. Still only in his mid-twenties he has the world at his feet and he looks sure to be in the engine room of the England scrum for some time to come. A gifted line-out jumper, a strong scrummager and a quick, athletic performer in the open, he has all the parts of a top lock forward.

# SCOTLAND

## BRYAN REDPATH

It has been a very difficult couple of seasons for Scotland, and the shortage of a large number of absolutely top-class players was highlighted by the selection of the Lions last year, when only a handful of Scots made the tour. The Scots have the advantage of being guided by the very best coach around in Ian McGeechan, but the lack of raw materials has made it very difficult to beat countries like England and France, who have great strength in depth. So the Scots need a few outstanding and experienced players to build their side around, and Bryan Redpath will be vitally important to them as they prepare for the World Cup. He won his first cap against New Zealand in 1993 and he has been a regular member of the squad since then. He played in the 1995 and 1999 World Cups and looks sure to be the number one scrum half for the 2003 tournament. He is a quick, accurate passer, sharp and explosive on the break, a gusty defender and a good kicker. He is competitive and he is just the player to inspire the new young blood in the Scottish team.

## SCOTT MURRAY

The Scottish pack has been noted more for mobility in the open and ability to win ruck after ruck driving forward than for any outstanding ability in set-piece play. The problem is that to perform really well in the open it is important to build on a decent set-piece platform. Against the heavyweights of world rugby the Scottish pack has seemed a little lightweight, but at least in the line out they have one of the best lock forwards in Europe in Scott Murray. To have any chance of making a serious impact in the Six Nations Championship, Scotland need to be guaranteed their own scrummage ball and their own line-out ball. Tom Smith and Gordon Bulloch look after the scrums while Scott Murray is fully capable of dominating the line out. He is a natural, athletic jumper who has played outstandingly well for Scotland since he won his first cap against Australia in 1997. He is a good scrummager and very mobile

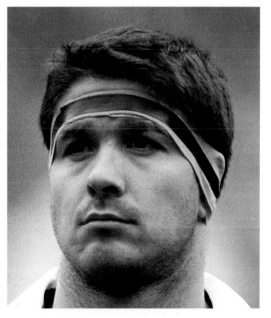

in the open, but he is above all a great line-out player. He was a little disappointing in 2001 with the Lions in Australia. Scotland desperately need him at his best in 2003.

# WALES

## IESTYN HARRIS

If one considers all the countries that have produced exciting backs in the past 30 years, Wales would be right up there with the best of them. Unfortunately the production line of great attacking runners which thrived in the 1970s and 1980s seemed to grind to a halt in the 1990s, with a handful of obvious exceptions like Jonathan Davies and Ieuan Evans. Now there is the real prospect of yet another star sidestepping all over the Millennium Stadium, leaving opponents snatching at shadows. Iestyn Harris first burst on the scene playing rugby league, but just as England and Australia are successfully recruiting players from the other code, so have Wales with Harris, who has made the transition to union in a relatively short time. He won his first cap after switching from Leeds Rhinos to Cardiff. He is a very talented player who with another season in union under his belt could well develop into one of the best backs to appear in the 2003 World Cup.

## MARTYN WILLIAMS

The Welsh pack has suffered in the Six Nations Championship against England, France and Ireland, and the big countries from the southern hemisphere – New Zealand, Australia and South Africa – all have the edge over Wales. It is fortunate that despite struggling occasionally in the set pieces they have a very good back row. Built around the formidable Scott Quinnell at No. 8, the unit can call on two or three excellent flankers, with Martyn Williams the best and now most influential. He first came to prominence with the Welsh Schoolboys team which beat Australia in 1994. He began his senior career with Pontypridd, helping them to win the league title in 1997. He won his first cap in 1996, and having switched to Cardiff he has now established himself in the Welsh team and will be a key player through to the 2003 World Cup. He went to Australia with the 2001 Lions and did not quite fulfil his potential, but

there is every likelihood that he will be a real force when he returns Down Under for the World Cup.

# IRELAND

## DAVID HUMPHREYS

The Irish team have enjoyed two good seasons, with the highlight unquestionably the magnificent victory over England in Dublin in October 2001. The big Irish victories tend to be a reflection of a tremendous team effort and there is no doubt this is a very strong Irish squad as we move into World Cup year. While France and England continue to dominate northern hemisphere rugby, Ireland have closed the gap quite considerably over the past year. One of their strengths is their half-back partnership of David Humphreys and Peter Stringer. Humphreys won his first cap against France in 1996 and he has been a prolific points scorer ever since. With over 40 caps he is very experienced, even though he has only recently established himself as first-choice fly half ahead of Ronan O'Gara. He is a consistent goal-kicker who regularly keeps the scoreboard ticking over and he is also a very good stand-off. He now has an exciting threequarter line outside him, and if the Irish forwards can continue their good form Humphreys can help to mastermind further Irish victories.

## ANTHONY FOLEY

Although he won his first cap against England back in 1995 and went on to play in nine Tests in the next two years, Anthony Foley then dropped out of the Irish side for the next three years. In 2000 he became a key player in the Munster side and he played so impressively he immediately re-established himself in the national team. He has been the first-choice No. 8 for the past three years and is an important figure in a very good back row. At the moment the Irish are blessed with several top-class loose forwards headed by David Wallace, Kieron Dawson and Eric Miller, as well as Foley himself. This has been the main strength of the Irish side because the tight-five forwards, with the exception of hooker Keith Wood, would not be considered as strong as those of England or France, and Ireland have remained so competitive through the exploits of their back row. Foley is similar in

style to Dean Richards and by doing all the hard graft he gives the flankers the opportunity to shine in the open. With a good back row and a steady pair of half backs Ireland can look forward to another good season.

# FRANCE

## FABIEN GALTHIE

The French have flattered to deceive in recent seasons, but in 2002 everything came right and they played some wonderful rugby to win the Six Nations Championship and complete the Grand Slam in the process. Great credit must go to Fabien Galthié their evergreen scrum half, who won his first cap for France against Romania 12 years ago in 1991 and now with 50 caps is far and away the most experienced of the French backs. He was in outstanding form in 2002, proving he is one of the very best scrum halves in world rugby. He is a great passer of the ball, a great reader of the game, he is devastating on the break and he is a tremendous captain. With so many of the current French backs relatively new to international rugby, it is very important that France can rely on their veteran star. He will be 34 years of age by the end of the 2003 Six Nations, but if France are to win the championship and do well in the World Cup they need one final great year from Galthié.

## IMANOL HARINORDOQUY

The French have had a rash of great back-row forwards in the past 30 years, from Jean-Pierre Bastiat and Walter Spanghero in the 1970s, to Jean-Pierre Rives in the 1980s, through to Abdel Benazzi and Olivier Magne in the 1990s. The 2002 Six Nations Championship saw the introduction of a 22-year-old No. 8 who just might go on to be yet another great back-row forward. Imanol Harinordoquy burst on to the international scene in 2002 with some outstanding performances in what turned out to be a brilliant French back row and arguably the best back row in world rugby. The Six Nations was won by the fantastic effort from those three players – Harinordoquy, Magne and Serge Betsen. They outplayed the English in Paris, and as a triumvirate they will be the key to French success in the immediate future. Harinordoquy is a big, strong forward and he is also fast and athletic in the open.

With a few more caps under his belt, he could well be one of the stars of the 2003 World Cup.

# ITALY

### ALESSANDRO TRONCON

Although Italy boast a lot of very good players they have only three or four who are really top class, and it is essential that these stars act as an inspiration to the rest of the team. Alessandro Troncon has been one of their very best backs over the past eight years since he won his first cap against Spain in 1994. He is an outstanding scrum half who has performed brilliantly for his French club Monteferrand and also for Italy. He is a quick, accurate passer, good on the break and he is very competitive in defence. He is the key man now in the Italian side, with a wealth of experience. He had 66 caps by the end of the 2002 Six Nations Championship and he took part in the 1995 and the 1999 World Cups. He has worked well with the Italian back row, especially Mauro Bergamasco, and he has enjoyed a wonderful half-back partnership with the legendary Diego Dominguez. He has the difficult task of having to play behind a beaten pack most of the time, but he is so talented and creative he is able to bring out the best in the rest of the Italian backs.

### ALESSANDRO MOSCARDI

The Italian team failed to win a match in the 2002 Six Nations Championship, but they still proved pretty competitive in every match and there is no doubt they have made steady progress since they first played in the championship in 2000. One of their biggest problems has been a lack of discipline which has meant they give away far too many penalties. There has been some improvement in the past 12 months, but there is a long way to go and the most important member of the Italian team in respect of maintaining discipline is the captain, Alessandro Moscardi. He is a very experienced player who won his first cap in 1993 and has now played over 40 times for Italy. He is one of the top hookers in European rugby – not just in set-piece play, he is also very good in the open. He leads by example and is highly respected by the rest of his team. He has the task of leading his forwards and inspiring them to be fiercely competitive and aggressive while not conceding any penalties.

# Fixtures 2002-03

**AUGUST 2002**

| | |
|---|---|
| Sat, 17th | Middlesex Charity Sevens |
| Fri, 30th/ | |
| Sat, 31st | Celtic League Pools A & B (1) |
| Sat, 31st | English Premiership (1) |
| | Eng Nat Lges 1,2,3N,3S (1) |
| | English Senior Cup Qual Round |
| | Scottish Premiership 1-3 (1) |
| | Scottish Nat Leagues 1-5 (1) |
| | Welsh Nat Lges 1,2,3W (1) |

**SEPTEMBER 2002**

| | |
|---|---|
| Fri, 6th/ | |
| Sat 7th | Celtic League Pools A & B (2) |
| Sat, 7th | English Premiership (2) |
| | Eng Nat Lges 1,2,3N,3S (2) |
| | Eng Nat Lges 12s (1) |
| | English Senior Cup Prelim Rd |
| | Scottish Premiership 1-3 (2) |
| | Scottish Cups Round One |
| | Welsh Nat Lges 1,2,3W (2) |
| | Welsh Nat Lge 3E (1) |
| Fri, 13th/ | |
| Sat, 14th | Celtic League Pools A & B (3) |
| Sat, 14th | English Premiership (3) |
| | Eng Nat Lges 1,2,3N,3S (3) |
| | Eng Nat Lges 12s (2)/10s (1) |
| | Scottish Premiership 1-3 (3) |
| | Scottish Nat Leagues 1-5 (2) |
| | Welsh Nat Lges 1,2,3W (3) |
| | Welsh Nat Lge 3E (2) |
| Fri, 20th/ | |
| Sat, 21st | Celtic League Pools A & B (4) |
| Sat, 21st | English Premiership (4) |
| | Eng Nat Lges 1 & 2 (4) |
| | English Senior Cup Round One |
| | English I'mediate Cup Rd One |
| | English Junior Cup Round One |
| | Scottish Premiership 1-3 (4) |
| | Scottish Nat Leagues 1-5 (3) |
| | Welsh Nat Lges 1 & 2 (4) |
| Wed, 24th | Welsh Nat Lge 1 (5) |
| Fri, 27th/ | |
| Sat, 28th | Celtic League Pools A & B (5) |
| Sat, 28th | English Premiership (5) |
| | Eng Nat Lges 1 & 2 (5) |
| | Eng Nat Lges 3N & 3S (4) |
| | Eng Nat Lges 12s (3)/10s (2) |
| | Scottish Premiership 1-3 (5) |
| | Scottish Nat Leagues 1-5 (4) |
| | Welsh Nat Lges 1 (6)/2 (5) |
| | Welsh Nat Lges 3W (4)/3E (3) |

**OCTOBER 2002**

| | |
|---|---|
| Fri, 4th/ | |
| Sat, 5th | Celtic League Pools A & B (6) |
| Sat, 5th | English Premiership (6) |
| | Eng Nat Lge 1 (6) |
| | Eng Nat Lges 12s (4)/10s (3) |
| | English Senior Cup Round Two |
| | Scottish Premiership 1-3 (6) |
| | Scottish Nat Leagues 1-5 (5) |
| | Welsh Nat Lges 1 (7)/2 (6) |
| | Welsh Nat Lges 3W (5)/3E (4) |
| Fri,11th/ | Heineken Cup Round One |
| Sun, 13th | Parker Pen Challenge Cup |
| | Round One (1st legs) |
| Sat, 12th | Eng Nat Lge 1 (7) |
| | Eng Nat Lge 2 (6) |
| | Eng Nat Lges 3N & 3S (5) |
| | Eng Nat Lges 12s (5)/10s (4) |
| | Scottish Premiership 1-3 (7) |
| | Scottish Cups Round Two |
| | Welsh Nat Lges 1 (8)/2 (7) |
| | Welsh Nat Lges 3W (6)/3E (5) |
| Fri, 18th/ | Heineken Cup Round Two |
| Sun,20th | Parker Pen Challenge Cup |
| | Round One (2nd legs) |
| Sat, 19th | Eng Nat Lges 3N & 3S (6) |
| | English Senior Cup Rd Three |
| | English I'mediate Cup Rd Two |
| | English Junior Cup Round Two |
| | Scottish Premiership 1-3 (8) |
| | Scottish Nat Leagues 1-5 (6) |
| | Welsh Nat Lges 1 (9)/2 (8) |
| | Welsh Nat Lge 3W (7) |
| | Welsh Challenge Cup |
| | (provisional) |
| Tue, 22nd | Welsh Nat Lge 1 (10) |
| Fri, 25th/ | |
| Sun, 27th | Celtic League Pools A & B (7) |
| Sat, 26th | English Premiership (7) |
| | Eng Nat Lge 1 (8) |
| | Eng Nat Lges 3N & 3S (7) |
| | Eng Nat Lges 12s (6)/10s (5) |
| | Irish Leagues 1,2,3 (1) |
| | Scottish Premiership 1-3 (9) |
| | Scottish Nat Leagues 1-5 (7) |
| | Welsh Nat Lges 1 (11)/2 (9) |
| | Welsh Nat Lges 3W (8)/3E (6) |
| Tue, 29th/ | |
| Wed, 30th | Welsh Premier League (1) |

**NOVEMBER 2002**

| | |
|---|---|
| Sat, 2nd | English Premiership (8) |
| | Eng Nat Lge 1 (9) |
| | Eng Nat Lges 2,3N,3S (8) |
| | Eng Nat Lges 12s (7)/10s (6) |
| | Irish Leagues 1,2,3 (2) |
| | Scottish Cups Round Three |
| | Welsh Premier League (2) |
| | Welsh Nat Lge 1 (12) |
| | Welsh Nat Lges 3W (9)/3E (7) |
| | Welsh Challenge Cup (prov) |

| | |
|---|---|
| Sat, 9th | ENGLAND v NEW ZEALAND |
| | IRELAND v AUSTRALIA |
| | SCOTLAND v ROMANIA |
| | WALES v FIJI |
| | English Premiership (9) |
| | Eng Nat Lges 3N & 3S (9) |
| | English Senior Cup Round Four |
| | English I'mediate Cup Rd Three |
| | English Junior Cup Rd Three |
| | Welsh Nat Lges 1 (13)/3E (8) |
| | Welsh Nat Lges 2,3W (10) |
| Sun, 10th | Scottish Premiership 1-3 (10) |
| | Scottish Nat Leagues 1-5 (8) |
| Tue, 12th | Scotland 'A' v South Africa |
| | Cmbd Services v Barbarians |
| Sat, 16th | ENGLAND v AUSTRALIA |
| | SCOTLAND v SOUTH AFRICA |
| | WALES v CANADA |
| | English Premiership (10) |
| | Eng Nat Lges 1,3N & 3s (10) |
| | Eng Nat Lge 2 (9) |
| | Eng Nat Lges 12s (8)/10s (7) |
| | Irish Leagues 1,2,3 (3) |
| | Welsh Nat Lge 1 (14) |
| | Welsh Nat Lges 2,3W (11) |
| Sun, 17th | IRELAND v FIJI |
| | Scottish Premiership 1-3 (11) |
| Wed. 20th | Scotland 'A' v Fiji |
| Sat, 23rd | ENGLAND v SOUTH AFRICA |
| | IRELAND v ARGENTINA |
| | WALES v NEW ZEALAND |
| | English Premiership (11) |
| | Eng Nat Lges 1,3N & 3S (11) |
| | Eng Nat Lge 2 (10) |
| | Eng Nat Lges 12s (9) |
| | Scottish Premiership 1-3 (12) |
| | Scottish Nat Leagues 1-5 (9) |
| | Welsh Nat Lge 1 (15) |
| Sun, 24th | SCOTLAND v FIJI |
| | Irish League 1 (4) |
| Fri, 29th/ | |
| Sun, 1st | Celtic League Quarter-finals |
| Sat, 30th | NORTH v SOUTH (Cardiff) |
| | English Premiership (12) |
| | Eng Nat Lge 2 (11) |
| | Eng Nat Lges 3N & 3S (12) |
| | Eng Nat Lges 12s (10)/10s (8) |
| | English Senior Cup Round Five |
| | English I'mediate Cup Rd Four |
| | England Junior Cup Rd Four |
| | Irish League 1 (4 continued) |
| | Irish Leagues 2 & 3 (4) |
| | Scottish Premiership 1-3 (13) |
| | Scottish Nat Leagues 1-5 (10) |
| | Welsh Nat Lges 1 (16)/3E (9) |
| | Welsh Nat Lges 2,3W (12) |
| | Welsh Challenge Cup (prov) |

## DECEMBER 2002

| | |
|---|---|
| Fri, 6th/ | Heineken Cup Round Three |
| Sun, 8th | Parker Pen Challenge Cup |
| | Round Two (1st legs) |

| | |
|---|---|
| | Parker Pen Shield |
| | Round One (1st legs) |
| Sat, 7th | Eng Nat Lges 1 & 2 (12) |
| | Eng Nat Lges 3N & 3S (13) |
| | Eng Nat Lges 12s (11)/10s (9) |
| | Irish Leagues 1,2,3 (5) |
| | Scottish Premiership 1-3 (14) |
| | Scottish Nat Leagues 1-5 (11) |
| | Welsh Nat Lges 1 (17)/3E (10) |
| | Welsh Nat Lges 2,3W (13) |
| Tue, 10th | OXFORD v CAMBRIDGE |
| | Oxford U21 v Cambridge U21 |
| Fri,13th/ | Heineken Cup Round Four |
| Sun, 15th | Parker Pen Challenge Cup |
| | Round Two (2nd legs) |
| | Parker Pen Shield |
| | Round One (2nd legs) |
| Sat, 14th | Eng Nat Lges 1 & 2 (13) |
| | Eng Nat Lges 3N & 3S (14) |
| | Eng Nat Lges 12s (12)/10s (10) |
| | Irish Leagues 2 & 3 (6) |
| | Scottish Cups Round Four |
| | Welsh Nat Lges 1 (18)/3E (11) |
| | Welsh Nat Lges 2,3W (14) |
| Sat, 21st | Eng Nat Lge 2 (14) |
| | Eng Nat Lges 3N & 3S (15) |
| | Eng Nat Lges 12s (13) |
| | English Senior Cup Round Six |
| | English I'mediate Cup Rd Five |
| | English Junior Cup Round Five |
| | Scottish Premiership 1-3 (15) |
| | Welsh Premier League (3) |
| | Welsh Nat Lges 2,3W (15) |
| | Welsh Nat Lge 3E (12) |
| | Welsh Challenge Cup (prov) |
| Thu, 26th | Welsh Premier League (4) |
| Sat, 28th | English Premiership (13) |
| | Irish League 1 (6) |
| | Welsh Nat Lges 1 (19)/3E (13) |
| | Welsh Nat Lges 2,3W (16) |
| Sun, 29th/ | |
| Mon, 30th | Welsh Premier League (5) |

## JANUARY 2003

| | |
|---|---|
| Sat, 4th/ | |
| Sun, 5th | Celtic League Semi-finals |
| Sat, 4th | English Premiership (14) |
| | Eng Nat Lge 1 (14) |
| | Eng Nat Lge 2 (15) |
| | Eng Nat Lges 3N & 3S (16) |
| | Eng Nat Lges 12s (14)/10s (11) |
| | Irish Leagues 2 & 3 (7) |
| | Scottish Premiership 1-3 (16) |
| | Scottish Nat Leagues 1-5 (12) |
| | Welsh Premier League (6) |
| | Welsh Nat Lges 1 (20)/3E (14) |
| | Welsh Nat Lges 2,3W (17) |
| Fri,10th/ | Heineken Cup Round Five |
| Sun, 12th | Parker Pen Challenge Cup |
| | Q-finals (1st legs) |
| | Parker Pen Shield |
| | Q-finals (1st legs) |

| | | | |
|---|---|---|---|
| Sat, 11th | Eng Nat Lge 1 (15) | | Scottish Nat Leagues 1-5 (15) |
| | Eng Nat Lge 2 (16) | | Welsh Nat Lges 1 (24)/3E (19) |
| | Eng Nat Lges 3N & 3S (17) | | Welsh Nat Lges 2,3W (22) |
| | Eng Nat Lges 12s (15) | Fri, 14th | England 'A' v France 'A' |
| | Irish Leagues 2 & 3 (8) | | England U21 v France U21 |
| | Scottish Cups Round Five | | Italy 'A' v Wales 'A' |
| | Welsh Nat Lges 1 (21)/3E (15) | | Italy U21 v Wales U21 |
| | Welsh Nat Lges 2,3W (18) | | Scotland 'A' v Ireland 'A' |
| Fri, 17th/ | Heineken Cup Round Six | | Scotland U21 v Ireland U21 |
| Sun, 19th | Parker Pen Challenge Cup | Sat, 15th | ENGLAND v FRANCE |
| |         Q-finals (2nd legs) | | ITALY v WALES |
| | Parker Pen Shield | | SCOTLAND v IRELAND |
| |         Q-finals (2nd legs) | | Scottish Nat Leagues 1-5 (16) |
| Sat, 18th | Eng Nat Lge 1 (16) | Wed, 19th | Welsh Nat Lge 1 (25) |
| | Eng Nat Lge 2 (17) | Fri, 21st | France 'A' v Scotland 'A' |
| | Eng Nat Lges 3N & 3S (18) | | France U21 v Scotland U21 |
| | Eng Nat Lges 12s (16)/10s (12) | | Italy 'A' v Ireland 'A' |
| | English I'mediate Cup Rd Six | | Italy U21 v Ireland U21 |
| | English Junior Cup Round Six | | Wales 'A' v England 'A' |
| | Irish League 1 (7) | | Wales U21 v England U21 |
| | Dublin U v Malone (Irish Lge 3) | Sat, 22nd | FRANCE v SCOTLAND |
| | Scottish Premiership 1-3 (17) | | ITALY v IRELAND |
| | Scottish Nat Leagues 1-5 (13) | | WALES v ENGLAND |
| | Welsh Nat Lges 1 (22)/3E (16) | | Eng Nat Lge 1 (20) |
| | Welsh Nat Lges 2,3W (19) | | Eng Nat Lge 2 (21) |
| Sat, 25th | Eng Nat Lge 1 (17) | | Eng Nat Lges 3N & 3S (22) |
| | Eng Nat Lge 2 (18) | | English I'mediate Cup Q-finals |
| | Eng Nat Lges 3N & 3S (19) | | English Junior Cup Q-finals |
| | English Senior Cup Q-finals | | |
| | Irish League 1 (8) | **MARCH 2003** | |
| | Irish Leagues 2 & 3 (9) | Sat, 1st | English Premiership (17) |
| | Scottish Premiership 1-3 (18) | | Eng Nat Lge 1 (21) |
| | Scottish Nat Leagues 1-5 (14) | | Eng Nat Lge 2 (22) |
| | Welsh Premier League (7) | | Eng Nat Lges 3N & 3S (23) |
| | Welsh Nat Lges 2,3W (20) | | Eng Nat Lges 12s (19)/10s (15) |
| | Welsh Nat Lge 3E (17) | | English Senior Cup Semi-finals |
| | Welsh Challenge Cup (prov) | | English Challenge Shield S-finals |
| | | | Irish League 1 (11) |
| **FEBRUARY 2003** | | | Irish Leagues 2 & 3 (12) |
| Sat, 1st | English Premiership (15) | | Scottish Nat Leagues 1-5 (17) |
| | Eng Nat Lge 1 (18) | | Welsh Premier League (10) |
| | Eng Nat Lge 2 (19) | | Welsh Nat Lges 1 (26)/3E (20) |
| | Eng Nat Lges 3N & 3S (20) | | Welsh Nat Lges 2,3W (23) |
| | Eng Nat Lges 12s (17)/10s (13) | Wed, 5th | Welsh Nat Lge 1 (27) |
| | Irish League 1 (9) | Fri, 7th | England 'A' v Italy 'A' |
| | Irish Leagues 2 & 3 (10) | | England U21 v Italy U21 |
| | Scottish Cups Quarter-finals | | Ireland 'A' v France 'A' |
| | Welsh Premier League (8) | | Ireland U21 v France U21 |
| | Welsh Nat Lges 1 (23)/3E (18) | | Scotland 'A' v Wales 'A' |
| | Welsh Nat Lges 2,3W (21) | | Scotland U21 v Wales U21 |
| Tue, 4th/ | | Sat, 8th | ENGLAND v ITALY |
| Wed, 5th | Welsh Premier League (9) | | IRELAND v FRANCE |
| Sat, 8th | English Premiership (16) | | SCOTLAND v WALES |
| | Eng Nat Lge 1 (19) | Sat, 15th | English Premiership (18) |
| | Eng Nat Lge 2 (20) | | Eng Nat Lge 1 (22) |
| | Eng Nat Lges 3N & 3S (21) | | Eng Nat Lge 2 (23) |
| | Eng Nat Lges 12s (18)/10s (14) | | Eng Nat Lges 3N & 3S (24) |
| | Celtic League Final | | Eng Nat Lges 12s (20)/10s (16) |
| | Irish League 1 (10) | | English I'mediate Cup S-finals |
| | Irish Leagues 2 & 3 (11) | | English Junior Cup Semi-finals |
| | Scottish Premiership stand-by | | Irish League 1 (12) |

|  |  |
|---|---|
| | Irish Leagues 2 & 3 (13) |
| | Scottish Nat Leagues 1-5 (18) |
| | Welsh Nat Lges 1 (28)/3E (21) |
| | Welsh Nat Lges 2,3W (24) |
| Fri, 21st | England 'A' v Scotland 'A' |
| | England U21 v Scotland U21 |
| | Italy 'A' v France 'A' |
| | Italy U21 v France U21 |
| | Wales 'A' v Ireland 'A' |
| | Wales U21 v Ireland U21 |
| Sat, 22nd | ENGLAND v SCOTLAND |
| | ITALY v FRANCE |
| | WALES v IRELAND |
| Fri, 28th | France 'A' v Wales 'A' |
| | France U21 v Wales U21 |
| | Ireland 'A' v England 'A' |
| | Ireland U21 v England U21 |
| | Scotland 'A' v Italy 'A' |
| | Scotland U21 v Italy U21 |
| Sat, 29th | FRANCE v WALES |
| | IRELAND v ENGLAND |
| | SCOTLAND v ITALY |
| | Eng Nat Lge 1 (23) |
| | Eng Nat Lge 2 (24) |
| | Eng Nat Lges 3N & 3S (25) |
| | Eng Nat Lges 12s (21)/10s (17) |

**APRIL 2002**

|  |  |
|---|---|
| Sat, 5th | English Cups Finals Day |
| | Irish League 1 (13) |
| | Irish Leagues 2 & 3 (14) |
| | Scottish Cups Semi-finals |
| | Welsh Challenge Cup Q-f (prov) |
| | Welsh Premier League (11) |
| | Welsh Nat Lges 1 (29)/3E (22) |
| | Welsh Nat Lges 2,3W (25) |
| Wed, 9th | Royal Air Force v Royal Navy |
| Fri,11th/ | Heineken Cup Quarter-finals |
| Sun, 13th | Parker Pen Challenge Cup |
| | Semi-finals (1st legs) |
| | Parker Pen Shield Semi-finals |
| | (1st legs) |
| Sat, 12th | English Premiership (19) |
| | Eng Nat Lge 1 (24) |
| | Eng Nat Lge 2 (25) |
| | Eng Nat Lges 3N & 3S (26) |
| | Eng Nat Lges 12s (22)/10s (18) |
| | English National U20 Q-finals |
| | Irish League 1 (14) |
| | Monkstown v City of Derry |
| | (Irish Lge 3) |
| | Welsh Premier League (12) |
| | Welsh Nat Lges 1 (30)/3E (23) |
| | Welsh Nat Lges 2,3W (26) |
| Sat, 19th | English Premiership (20) |
| | Eng Nat Lge 1 (25) |
| | Irish League 1,2,3 (15) |
| | Welsh Nat Lges 1 (31)/3E (24) |
| | Welsh Nat Lges 2,3W (27) |
| Tue, 22nd/ | |
| Wed, 23rd | Welsh Premier League (13) |

|  |  |
|---|---|
| Sat,26th/ | Heineken Cup Semi-finals |
| Sun 27th | Parker Pen Challenge Cup |
| | Semi-finals (2nd legs) |
| | Parker Pen Shield Semi-finals |
| | (2nd legs) |
| Sat, 26th | Eng Nat Lges 1 & 2 (26) |
| | Eng Nat Lges 3N, 3S Play-offs |
| | Eng Nat Lges 12s/10s Play-offs |
| | County Shield Round 1 |
| | Scottish Cups Finals Day |
| | Welsh Challenge Cup S-f (prov) |
| | Welsh Premier League (14) |
| | Welsh Nat Lges 1 (32)/3E (25) |
| | Welsh Nat Lges 2,3W (28) |
| Tue, 29th | Army v Royal Air Force |

**MAY 2002**

|  |  |
|---|---|
| Sat, 3rd | English Premiership (21) |
| | Royal Navy v Army |
| | County Championships Rd One |
| | County Shield Round Two |
| | Welsh Premier League (15) |
| | Welsh Nat Lges 1 (33)/3E (26) |
| | Welsh Nat Lges 2,3W (29) |
| Tue, 6th/ | |
| Wed, 7th | Welsh Premier League (16) |
| Sat, 10th | English Premiership (22) |
| | County Championships Q-finals |
| | County Shield Semi-finals |
| | Welsh Premier League (17; prov) |
| | Welsh Nat Lge 1 (34) |
| | Welsh Nat Lges 2,3W (30) |
| Tue, 13th | E Midlands v Barbarians (prov) |
| Sat, 17th | English Premiership Play-offs |
| | County Ch'ships & Shield S-f |
| | Welsh Premier League (17; prov) |
| Fri, 23rd | Parker Pen Shield Final (prov) |
| Sat, 24th | Heineken Cup Final |
| | County Championships Play-offs |
| | Welsh Premier League (18) |
| Sun, 25th | ENGLAND v BARBARIANS |
| | Parker Challenge Cup Final |
| Tue, 27th | WALES v BARBARIANS |
| Sat, 31st | SCOTLAND v BARBARIANS |
| | Welsh Challenge Cup Final (prov) |
| | English Premier Ch'ship S-finals |
| | County Ch'ships & Shield Finals |

**JUNE 2002**

|  |  |
|---|---|
| Sat, 7th | English Premier Ch'ship Final |

*NB: Scottish National League stand-by dates – 7th September, 12th October, 2nd November, 14th December 2002; 11th January, 1st February, 5th April, 26th April 2003.*

Mission Statement

The Wooden Spoon Society aims to enhance the quality and prospect of life for children and young persons in the United Kingdom who are presently disadvantaged either physically, mentally or socially

Charity Registration No: 326691